SO YOU WANT TO BE A TALENT AGENT?

EVERYTHING YOU NEED TO KNOW TO START YOUR OWN LOCAL TALENT BOOKING AGENCY

TOM "WOLF" ELLIOTT

iUniverse, Inc.
New York Bloomington

So You Want to Be a Talent Agent?
Everything You Need to Know to Start Your Own Local Talent Booking Agency

Tom Elliott Productions
P. O. Box 540441
Waltham, MA 02454-0441
(781) 647-2825

iUniverse books may be ordered through booksellers or by contacting:

iUniverse
1663 Liberty Drive
Bloomington, IN 47403
www.iuniverse.com
1-800-Authors (1-800-288-4677)

ISBN: 978-1-4502-2722-3 (sc)
ISBN: 978-1-4502-2723-0 (ebook)

Printed in the United States of America

iUniverse rev. date: 05/03/2010

Table of Contents

List of Tables

List of Illustrations

Foreword

I am Marianne Windham, President of Windham Entertainment, Inc. It is both an honor and a privilege to be able to share a few comments about how grateful Windham Entertainment is to Tom Elliott of Tom Elliott Productions for his book, *So You Want to Be a Talent Agent?* (originally titled, *Clowns, Clients, and Chaos - Starting a Hometown Talent Agency for Fun and Profit)*. My husband, Darin, and I opened our Southeast talent agency in 2004; and we consider Tom to be one of the biggest inspirations in starting our business.

Darin and I had both been entertainers for most of our lives. This personal passion and involvement in the performing arts had given us a unique perspective in the entertainment business. In addition, during the course of our careers in corporate sales and marketing, we recognized a growing need for a business to represent the many talented individuals in our region to the corporate world. This business could assist other businesses and private individuals in acquiring the appropriate entertainment for most any event or celebration.

Plato said that "Necessity is the mother of invention." Windham Entertainment could not agree more. Due to the overwhelming number of requests for talent that Darin and I had received for many years, we decided to embrace the idea that we had become the "go to" entertainment people in our region. We decided to start a talent agency! Though we are both determined and driven, we pictured ourselves jumping off a cliff and praying that there would either be a net to catch us or that we would grow wings! And so we began searching resources within the industry in order to lay the ground work for a successful business venture. At the same time, we were hoping that we would not have to "reinvent the wheel." And along came Tom Elliott.

Fortunately for us, I found Tom's book. As the title page states, this book most certainly includes "everything you need to know to start your own talent agency". It is packed full with detailed information from prospecting and promotion to policies and procedures. At the time that I purchased the book, I also had the opportunity to speak with Tom on the phone. He was so genuinely interested in our success, and I told him that I would keep him posted on our progress.

Jump four years ahead. Windham Entertainment, Inc. is still going strong, and growing every year. Windham Entertainment is a unique business and one that fills many needs in not only our own community, but we have now gained recognition as both a regional and national entertainment booking agency. Our roster includes people from across the nation - bands, solo artists and musicians, tribute artists and look-alikes, actors and models, magicians & unique circus acts, speakers and celebrities. Both our clients and our roster of talent come from not only our region - Alabama, Georgia, Tennessee, Florida - but also from California, New York, Texas, Washington, D.C., etc...We continue to use the jewels of wisdom that Tom has given us through this guide, right down to verbiage on forms and contracts included in his invaluable "manual". In April of 2008, Darin and I visited Boston and had the pleasure of meeting with Tom in person; and we continue to stay in touch. We are thrilled to be in the business of promoting FUN, and will be forever appreciative of Tom Elliott's contributions to our continued success. Thank you Tom!

Marianne Cook Windham
President, Windham Entertainment, Inc.
www.windhamentertainment.com

Preface

I recently read that the problem with some people is that they search endlessly for a job or career the same way that others seek that elusively perfect mate: looking for Mr. or Ms. Right, never finding it, and being constantly frustrated and despondent.

Well, in my opinion, I think that the problem is that people settle *too* easily—for a job that's "just good enough". One that makes them hate facing the dawn every work day, one that's mind-deadening and energy-sucking.

What if *you* could find that "Prince (or Princess) Charming" career—a career that offers excitement, adequate compensation for your efforts, growth, challenge, and even a touch of glamour? Being a talent booking agent just might fill that bill …

People are different, and maybe being a talent agent isn't for everyone, but for most people it sure beats the paper-pushing, bureaucratic drudgery of most jobs. I've certainly enjoyed doing what I've been doing these last 30+ years, and I think you might, too.

This book will tell you *everything* you need to know about the talent booking business, talking you through every step of the process of setting up the business, finding your first talent and your first customers, and handling the scheduling, negotiating, contract-signing, and follow-up. And I've included several helpful appendices to lead you to suppliers, professional organizations and resources, and further reading.

Not only that, it can lead you down other paths as it did me—modeling agent, record producer, TV producer, artist manager, script writer, radio program guest slots, "movie star", and ghosthunter.

ENJOY!!!

Chapter 1
Getting Started

A Little Background...

Rather than do my own boasting, I'll let others do it for me:

"Back in the mid-70s, a young, hotshot computer programmer developed a crush on a Cambridge street singer named RuthAnna. With typical hacker's ingenuity, he figured the best way to meet her was to offer his services as her manager. He did. The relationship bloomed and before long, word was out among her performer friends that Tom Elliott was the man to see if you were an artist who needed an agent. ...

"Before the year ended, he had acquired a stable of nearly 100 assorted novelty acts and was on his way to a nice income, handling such artists as Leonard Solomon and his Majestic Bellowphone, jester Alexander Feldman, a Fiddler and Dancing Bear, and of course, his old flame, RuthAnna. 'That's how it all started. It wasn't anything I'd planned - it just worked out,' Tom grinned as he sprawled his lean frame across the cushioned leather sofa in the livingroom of his Beacon Hill apartment. 'I call it a home-town talent agency, because it's a viable business wherever you happen to live. *Each* wedding, fair, festival, Fourth of July parade, sidewalk sale, fund-raiser, and shopping mall is a chance to book an act. They're all 'hometown events', and if you represent talent, they're prime sales opportunities. . .

"There's a real need for this kind of business in most communities because the big-time talent agencies aren't interested in supplying inexpensive entertainment for birthday parties, company picnics, or Boy Scout gatherings. And it's tough for people to track down such entertainment on their own, especially if they want professionals, not just Uncle Louie in the clown suit once a year."

— Jerry Vovscko, The Seattle WA Independent Times

"What do Cheezo the Clown, Sgt. Pepperoni's One-Man Band, UFO abductee Betty Hill, magician Peter Sosna, Gene Autry's sister Barbara, and sword-swallower Don Leslie have in common? The answer is simple - Tom Elliott, talent agent and crusader for the street performer.

Elliott, a 43-year-old *bon vivant* and jack-of-all-trades, sat in his Beacon Hill apartment, surrounded by colorful pamphlets, record albums, and other promotional paraphernalia. 'I specialize in one-of-a-kind acts, from sideshow attractions to street singers - odd-ball entertainment, in other words,' he said. Fiddlers, clowns, jazz bands, ventriloquists, puppeteers, jugglers, organ grinders, fire-eating unicyclists, tattooed men who swallow swords, magicians, Shakespearean actors, witches, ghost hunters - all are part of Elliott's playbill.

"What made Elliott, a self-made business executive, enter the world of entertainment? 'I fell helplessly in love with a street singer who sang on Boston Common a number of years ago,' he sighed. RuthAnna, a beautiful, fragile-looking blonde, played her guitar and sang for her supper in the days when street performing was illegal. In 1975, Elliott decided he was going to take the vulnerable flower child under his wing and help her produce a record album and perform in concert halls. Once Elliott captured his fair-haired maiden and started to promote her, suddenly he found himself with a dozen more street performers who asked if he'd do the same for them. From that start, his list of clients quickly swelled to 60 …"

— *Sheila Barth, Beverly-Peabody Times*

"…A small-scale agency like Elliott's has several things going for it. It requires no special schooling to run and little cash to start. Best of all, everything can be handled out of your home."

— *Entrepreneur*

"…A talent agency is one of the most exciting businesses in the world, and it can lead to some fascinating sidelines. Add a speakers' bureau or modeling subsidiary, produce record albums, sponsor concerts, produce a TV series, write articles and books about what you're doing. Can any other business offer so many opportunities?"

— *Income Opportunities*

"Elliott has done what many people only dream of: he has turned his hobby into a lucrative sideline. And he's become expert enough at agenting to write articles and books about it. Like a true entrepreneur he's never content to simply do one job at a time …

"Not all of Elliott's talent comes from the Boston area. One of his clients, for example, is the sister of Gene Autry, who lives in New Jersey and does a lasso act with her daughter. He once had Betty Hill, the New Hampshire woman who, along with her husband, was kidnapped and taken aboard a UFO back in the early 1960s, on his weekly cablevision series, *Personal Perspectives*. He's gone UFO hunting with her, and says he's seen a few - strange lights, anyway. But Elliott tends to get involved with his clients. And he recently visited a tattooed sword-swallower he books out of San Francisco, and came back with a tattoo himself. He hasn't tried sword-swallowing yet, but who knows?"

— *News West*

"Talent is a flame. Genius is a fire."

—*Wally Amos, of Famous Amos' Cookies*

So You Want to Be A Talent Agent?

Sure, it *sounds* good. But, you may ask, "Where do you think I live, Hollywood or New York?" However, let me ask you to just stop a minute and consider:

- The number of bands, orchestras, and trios your fellow <u>citizens</u> (not to mention bars, restaurants, lodges, clubs, retailers, and schools) hire each and every year for their weddings, anniversaries, proms, and other social events.
- The clowns, mimes, and magicians you've seen at company picnics, children's birthday parties, summer recreation programs, retail "grand openings", and sidewalk sales.
- The acts you've enjoyed at church suppers, local fund-raisers, and lodge gatherings.
- Those summer concerts and other programs sponsored by your municipality.
- All the weekly events at your local museums, libraries, civic centers, high school auditoriums, community colleges, and other institutions.
- The Fourth of July parades and other celebrations that take place each year in your city …

That's right - **entertainment is BIG business**, *even in small towns*. And because I firmly believe that *every* city and town needs someone to supply that entertainment to eager prospects, you can make it *your* business if you want to.

I'm Tom Elliott, owner and president of Tom Elliott Productions (TEP for short), and I've been in this business of entertainment since 1975. I have close to 200 regular clients, a number that increases every year, and I represent over 100 different acts.

I specialize in supplying talent to local arts and crafts festivals, municipal parks and recreation programs, shopping malls and other retailers, company picnics, private parties, weddings, museums, tourist attractions, and the like, all right in my town and surrounding communities. And I've also worked with clients half-way across the country and beyond.

I work at this venture only part-time, devoting anywhere from 10 to 15 hours weekly, and I've made it pay, mostly in towns with a population of under 30,000. It gives me a nice supplementary income, I've met a lot of fabulous people, and I've had a hell of a lot of fun to boot!

Like many would-be entrepreneurs, I've tried a number of different businesses—multi-level marketing, a bookstore, various mail order schemes—and I stayed with them two, possibly three years, tops, before I tired of them and boredom set in. They all had one thing in common—I could take them only so far. When I started TEP I thought it would be like all the others. But I've kept at it for over 30 years now and, even though I'm slowing down and in semi-retirement, I'm more enthusiastic about it than ever! And once *you've* been in the business a while, you'll feel the same way.

Is This for You?

I've aimed this book primarily at those of you who are thinking of starting a small-to-medium sized agency to handle the entertainment needs of your community and surrounding areas. I've oriented it away from the rock bands/nightclub booking arena and instead have focused on those less-competitive markets with which I'm more familiar and have had the most success.

One last thought before I begin: a lot of the advice I've included is given in the spirit of "Don't do as I do, do as I say". Believe me, I'm far from perfect when it comes to following my own recommendations; if I were, I'd be rich and retired by now. But maybe *you* can do better. If you can, I wish you all the success you deserve!

The Joys(?) and the Pains

Running a talent agency is one of the most diverse, challenging, exciting, and gratifying careers in all the world. Talent booking utilizes every ability, every experience, and every *talent* you possess. It's an opportunity that knows no limits in terms of how big you can grow, how famous you can become, how much money you can make, and into what directions you can expand. If you have the willingness to succeed, you're standing on the threshold of an unprecedented opportunity!

Unlike most other businesses, it costs very little in startup costs - a phone, a pencil, and a pad of paper are practically all you really need. And you won't have to spend money to rent an office or store front - you can run it right from your home.

Best of all, the buying and selling of talent is the heart of "show biz", with all its legendary glamour and glory. As an agent, you're a part of the heart-stirring rhythms of the carnival or circus you've booked into that vacant lot near the center of town, the breathtaking rising of the curtain on Opening Night at your civic center, the color and clamor of your town's Fourth-of-July parade, and the warmth and mellowness of the annual harvest festival on the village common - *because* you've *helped make each one possible.*

Are there pitfalls? Sure, every business opportunity has them. But with this one, you "choose your poison". Talent booking can be competitive, particularly if you're shooting to be a rock band promoter or represent big-name stars. You may encounter some tough customers—club owners who are frustratingly hard to reach, hard to sell, and harder yet to get to sign a binding contract. You may, depending on your market, run high legal and financial risks if a performer fails to show, a client cancels at the last minute, or an act is responsible for personal injury or property damage. On the other hand, if you stick to the low-pressure end of the spectrum, like booking clowns for birthday parties and sidewalk sales, you'll have little to worry about.

How Much Can You Expect to Earn?

As in any business, the amount of money to be made depends on a number of factors. To name just a few:

- The population of your area
- The affluence of its inhabitants
- How much time and effort you're willing to devote to the business.
- Your entertainment savvy and sales abilities
- What types of entertainment you handle
- How much money you can invest in advertising and promotion
- The overall economy

Of course, no one can guarantee you a certain income, but we can at least briefly discuss some of the parameters that could affect your potential:

» *Your Market Area*

Your **market area** should contain a population of at least 500,000 people, with a majority in the middle-to-upper-income class. Note that I'm not talking here about the population of the city or town where you live—I'm talking about your *metropolitan area* - the cluster of cities and towns that form your region and the geographic area to which the bulk of your advertising, mailings, and telephone solicitation will be targeted. You shouldn't find this to be a problem, because most of you live near a moderately large city. Besides, there are really no fixed geographic limits—the entire country can be your territory if you wish!

Just to prove that last point, I should mention that I've booked acts in Michigan, Louisiana, Pennsylvania, Illinois, Maine, Kentucky, and even California almost as easily as I do in the Greater Boston area. In fact, pitching an out-of-town act has a certain advantage. People become quickly bored with too much of the home-grown variety, and a new face is always an attraction. So, don't let distances stop you!

» *Types of Acts*

As you might expect, another factor that will determine your income is the type of acts you choose to handle. Obviously, a clown will generally pull down a substantially lower price than a 5-piece band. And a novice performer will earn a lot less than a seasoned performer or a celebrity.

» *Locale*

And, of course, the area of the country that you hail from is another piece of the puzzle. The Northeast and West Coast bring much higher prices than, let's say Boise, Idaho, but then competition is heavier and expenses are higher too. Again, you can leverage this by expanding your business to other areas of the country.

» *Calculating Your Potential Income*

If you stick to the birthday party/picnic/wedding circuits, you're going to be handling acts that charge anywhere from $125 (for a clown) to $500-1000 (for a band). Your commission will typically be 15% of these fees. (Some agencies charge 20% and a few charge 10%, but I happen to think that 15% is just about right.)

If you're starting out part-time (as most of you will be doing), and devoting the 10 to 12 hours per week I mentioned earlier, you should be able to place three or four acts a week. Assuming an average price of $300 apiece, that puts $180 a week (300x4x15%) into your pocket or close to $10,000 annually, and you can do a lot better than that during the holiday season.

On a full-time basis, you should be able to multiply these figures by at least a factor of four, giving you a gross income of $35,000 - $40,000 for your first year. Since many of your expenses are fixed, they won't rise proportionately with your gross income.

Remember—that's only for starters. I've conservatively based these estimates on relatively low-priced acts, marketed locally. This is a growing business, with a truly unlimited potential, and you can expand it any number of ways as you go along. It may sound like a bit of a cliché to say so, but "the sky's the limit". And when some of you are sitting poolside at your digs in Beverly Hills some day, you'll agree.

» *The Economy*

As with most businesses, talent booking is susceptible to the ups and downs of the local and national economies, and you should be prepared for some lean times now and then.

In recent years, we've all seen both the Federal and state governments drastically cut back on funding for the arts, and that impacts all public events. And local towns cut back, too, in hard times—if it's a choice between canceling those concerts at the bandstand this summer or laying off police or fire department personnel, you can guess which they'll choose.

The state of the economy also affects even the smallest of events—people aren't likely to want to spend $80 on a clown for their child's birthday party if they're having a hard time coming up with the mortgage payment.

So, if you've decided to jump in full-time, make sure you have a good-sized nest egg to see you through those dips and valleys, or can count on some alternative source of income.

Do You Have the "Right Stuff"?

Every career and every business has its own set of qualifications, and talent booking is no exception. But you'll find it somewhat unique in that its qualifications aren't as fixed or formal as those of other occupations.

Generally, colleges don't grant BS's or MBA's in talent booking, there are no tests or apprenticeships to pass for a license, and no previous experience is necessary. And, even more unusual, there's no right way to go about it. How you conduct your business can be as individualistic as you are. With the possible exception of door-to-door sales, talent booking is one of the last frontiers of old-fashioned rugged individualism.

So what are the qualifications? First there are the *basic* qualities that you should possess before you consider embarking on *any* business venture:

- **A desire to succeed**, and the self-discipline to stick to your goals.
- **A product or service which is different** from others in your marketing area, and which is needed.
- **Appropriate educational background and business experience**.
- **A willingness to take responsibility**.
- **A good organizer**, of yourself and others.
- The **stamina and ability** to devote the time and sweat necessary for success.
- **Support** of your immediate family.
- **Adequate resources** and credit.

Then there are the *special* qualities that I feel are especially valuable in *this* particular business. They mostly center on personality traits rather than academic degrees or job history. As I see it, you should:

- **Love people.** This is a people-oriented business, and you'll be dealing with a lot of them. Most times, you'll feel like you're caught right in between them! You'll need to be concerned for the well-being of both your client and your acts. You'll need to know the strengths and weaknesses of each entertainer and be ready to offer support when needed.

- **Be scrupulously honest**. Talent agents, like used-car salesmen and sideshow barkers, have a bad rep. So set yourself apart from the crowd. Your *clients* pay for and have a right to expect (a) an honest description of what they're buying, (b) quality entertainment as represented, and (c) fair and equitable rates. Your *performers*, in turn, expect you to (a) represent them with integrity, (b) do your best to ensure that all their requirements are met, and (c) pay them fully and promptly. Also be aware that you'll be handling a good deal of money, and you're responsible to see that every cent of it goes in the right pocket.

- **Be well-organized and attentive to detail.** This is extremely important in the talent business. You'll be juggling dozens of dates, times, places, names, fees, and arrangements, and one slip-up can spell disaster for both the client and the performer. Yes, everyone makes a mistake now and then, but in this venue more than any other, it can be both embarrassing and costly.

- **Believe in yourself and what you're selling.** Don't try to be a smooth talker, just be confident and knowledgeable about your offerings and present your performers to your clients with enthusiasm seasoned with imagination and down-to-earth honesty.

- **Be creative.** Talent booking is, to a large extent, promotional. You'll be challenged over and over again to come up with new ways to satisfy a client's specific needs, give advice to performers on how to improve their act and further their careers, and gain wider exposure for your agency. Talent booking is one field that doesn't award success to the pedestrian or the mediocre.

- **And above all, persevere.** The single most essential ingredient to success in this business is perseverance. Keep calling, keep mailing, keep knocking on doors, keep scouting for new acts, and do whatever else you have to do. Don't become discouraged easily. Your efforts will gradually produce a cumulative effect.

That's about all you need for starters (along with the pencil, paper, and telephone, of course). The rest comes with experience, and the only way to get experience in this business is to do it!

How Much Will It Cost to Start?

No one should choose a business just because it's cheap to set up, but this business *does* offer this benefit as an added bonus. You can start your agency with very little out-of-pocket money—actually for little more than the down payment on a new car! If you're starting out part-time, you'll certainly need no more than $1000 cash-in-hand to pay your expenses until the commissions start rolling in. Now how many businesses can you name that require that small an investment?

Of course if you're trying to break in on a full-time basis, you're going to need some support to feed, clothe, and shelter you for the first six months or so.

» *A Phone, a Pad, and a Pencil...*

Here's a list of the things you'll need and their estimated cost (don't forget to allow for any inflationary increases that might have occurred since this book was published):

7

Table 1. Start-up Costs

Item	Approx. Cost	Notes
Telephone and answering machine	$50-$175	Price depends on whether you purchase them separately or buy a combined unit, whether the phone is a portable, etc.
Computer System, Nonitor, Multi-function Printer, basic software	$700-1,200	Today you can purchase a first-class business computer system for well under $1000, including PC, printer, and monitor (see below).
Letterheads & envelopes (1,000)	$75-100	First impressions count, so don't stint.
Mailing labels (1,000)	$50	
Contract forms (500)	$25	
Business cards (1,000)	$50	
Advertising/Marketing/Promotion	-	See below.
Licensing and Bonding Fees	-	See below.
Insurance	-	See below

» *Printing*

As you can see, a good portion of your investment is in printed materials (sales collateral). Shop around—there are many good mail-order printing firms that offer real bargains, especially if you take advantage of their special first-timer offers. And, if you buy a computer, you can print many of these items yourself!

» *Office Equipment*

You can buy the typewriter and answering machine new or used. The answering machine should have a remote call-in feature so you can pick up your messages from any phone. That way, you can call in from your full-time job, keep on top of any calls that came in while you were at work, and hopefully return the calls during business hours that same day. Even better, you can pay a bit extra for your phone carrier's answering service, which at the moment runs somewhere around $3/month.

» *Computer System*

If you can possibly afford one, a computer system is a valuable tool, not only for the usual letter writing, but it's great for desktop publishing of your sales literature and business cards, for keeping track of sales contacts and maintaining mailing lists, doing your bookkeeping and filling out your tax returns, and reminding you of appointments, bookings, and other matters of import.

A complete system, with sufficient power "under the hood", and a high quality multifunction printer (print, copy, scan, fax), will run you well under $1000. One good bet is a line of computers known as e-Machines—good, basic computers at very reasonable prices.

Here's the minimal configuration I suggest (and remember that computer prices, contrary to most other things, continue to fall):

- PC with 3 GHertz speed and an up-to-date operating system (Windows XP, Windows Vista, or Windows7)
- 1 GB of random access memory (RAM)

- 260 GB (or more) hard drive
- Monitor of your choice
- Multifunction printer (print, copy, scan, fax)

If you can afford more than this, you can't go wrong buying more hard disk capacity or upping the speed. Many systems come with Windows, plus some sort of all-in-1 office software package (word processing, graphics, spreadsheet, etc.) already installed, so you shouldn't have to buy any software right away. Another item to consider is an external disk drive for backup.

Frankly, a going business can't afford *not* to have a computer these days! But you may be asking yourself whether you can carry the cost of a computer. There *is* a way— *business leasing*, and it's easy to arrange it if you have a good personal credit record. Yes, it may be a lease, but at the end of the three years you can choose to pay an additional amount (usually equal to around 10% of the total price), and the computer is *yours*, free and clear!

» *Advertising/Marketing/Promotion*

How much you spend (website, print, radio, TV, direct mail, etc.) depends on how fast you want to build up your roster of acts (see Chapter 3) and how you plan to find jobs for them (see Chapter 4). Generally, it's a good idea to put aside a fixed percentage of your earnings for these items—perhaps 10-15% to start. If you plan to use telemarketing and cold-calling primarily, then you can get by with a small advertising budget.

Legalities and Liabilities

At some point you're going to have to deal with the powers that be—your local, state, and federal governments. Registration, licensing, and bonding regulations vary from state to state, so check with the appropriate officials to find out the specific requirements. And then there's insurance. For now, I'll just explain some of the things you must consider.

» *Registering with the Town Clerk*

At the very least, you are required to register your business with the Town Clerk and obtain a Business Certificate. One reason for doing this is to provide a public record of who is behind your business name. Then, if someone has a complaint about your firm, and you're operating under a name other than your own (referred to as "doing business as" or "d.b.a."), they can call City Hall and find out who to contact, collect from, or sue. Fortunately, a business certificate usually costs no more than $15 or $20.

In some towns, you'll also have to check in with the building inspector and zoning board to determine if your house or apartment is zoned for an in-home business. One way to get around this is to use a Post Office box or mail drop as your legal business address. Even though it's obvious that you're not actually running your business out of a box, having one satisfies the letter of the law in this regard. Besides, it's always advisable (and safer) to use a mailing address that's not your private domicile. Moderate-sized post office boxes run around $75 annually.

So, talk to your municipal officials about the legal requirements of your city or town, and make sure you know what's required.

» *Licensing and Bonding*

Some states require that talent agents and managers be *licensed* (or registered) and/or *bonded*, the same as real estate brokers, insurance sales people, and others who represent people or property, and who collect money on behalf of others. New York and California are known to have some of the strictest regulations in the country. And some states may also require an employment agency license.

In those states requiring a license, the annual fee can run from $200 up to $600 or more. But more cumbersome is the paperwork required. You may have to provide copies of all your contracts and other standard forms, papers substantiating your trade name and incorporation (if applicable), and a bunch of other documentation.

By the way, unlike electricians and plumbers, licensing is nothing more than paying a fee for a piece of paper that says you can legitimately engage in the booking and managing of talent. It doesn't involve passing a competency test or meeting other criteria—it's just another convenient and legal way of getting more money out of your wallet.

Bonding is a kind of liability insurance. For a modest fee each year, a bonding company will insure you for a specified amount to cover anyone you might victimize by absconding with the funds. Required bonds can range from $500 (Kansas) up to $100,000 (Washington DC), but fortunately bonding is relatively inexpensive.

You might also be required to set up an escrow account at a bank, separate from all other business and personal checking or savings accounts, for holding advance payments from clients that will subsequently be paid to your performers.

» *Sales and Service Taxes*

In those states, counties, and cities that impose sales and/or services taxes, you will also have to register with the sales tax authorities and obtain a Sales Tax Certificate.

In locations where the only tax is on the sale of goods, you will have to collect and remit taxes only if you sell videos, CDs, T-shirts, books, or other merchandise.

In places where both goods *and* services are taxed, all performance fees are subject to the tax, and like sales taxes, *must be collected from the purchaser* and then passed on to the city or state. Such taxes are in addition to the city, state, and federal income taxes that you and your performers must pay on earnings.

Again, check with the appropriate officials about your obligations in this area.

» *Federal, State, and Local Income Taxes*

As a business, you are of course responsible for filing a business tax return (Schedule C) at both the federal and state levels (and possibly county and city as well). If you've set up your agency as a corporation, there are other forms and returns for which you're responsible.

Also, unless you're having enough tax withheld from your payroll check by your full-time employer to cover your agency earnings as well, you may have to file and pay a Quarterly Estimated Income Tax. And, if the agency is your full-time job and only source of income, you'll also have to pay a Self-Employment Tax (akin to the FICA deduction by an employer).

Finally, if you employ other people, you may be obligated to pay premiums for Workingmen's Compensation, to cover injuries on the job, health insurance premiums, and other fees.

Since performers are, by law, generally considered to be independent contractors and not employees of your agency or your clients, neither you nor your clients are required to deduct any moneys from their earnings. However, being self-employed, *they* are responsible for filing Quarterly Estimated Income Tax returns, paying self-employment taxes (if they're not employed at other jobs), etc., on their own behalf

» *Insurance*

Although it's not obligatory, you may, as a precaution, want to consider the purchase of several kinds of **insurance**:

- **Business liability insurance**, to protect you against potential claims that might be brought against you. For example, if you meet clients at your home (or office), you might want insurance to cover you if they should be injured on the premises. Other special riders can protect you against suits for libel, cancellations, and damages incurred due to non-performance or negligence.
- **Legal insurance**, to pay partially or in full for attorneys and other legal costs you might incur.
- **Personal insurance** (medical, dental, disability, life) to protect yourself and your family against unexpected illnesses and accidents.
- **Home and/or office insurance**, to cover you in the event of fire, theft, or other disasters. *Be aware that your homeowners policy may not compensate you for loss of business equipment if they can prove that you were using your home as an office.* Also, many policies do not cover computers and other expensive office equipment unless you've purchased additional coverage for those items, nor do they cover loss of cash or other negotiable securities.
- **Additional automobile insurance**, if you use the car for agency business. Like your homeowner's insurance, your ordinary auto policy may not cover you if you use your car for business and have not so notified your insurance company.
- **Equipment repair contracts**, to pay for repairs to computers, copiers, and other equipment in event of breakdowns. Usually such contracts (sometimes called "extended warranties") are not cost effective, and you'd be better off socking away the premiums into your own account.

Self-Education and Self-Improvement

Dry words perhaps, but if you're *really* interested in the wide, wild world of entertainment (and you should be, or you should maybe consider another line of business), running a talent agency can be an ongoing education.

You'll never stop learning. The more you know, the more you'll enjoy working with your performers, the more you'll appreciate their unique talents, and the more directions you can choose to go (see Chapter 7). Over the past decade and a half, I've delved quite deeply into Shakespeare, fire-eating, mountain dulcimers, Capuchin monkeys, sword-swallowing, sound studio engineering, hypnotism, TV production, and about 100 other subjects.

I personally subscribe to the theory that this big old world is one humungous university, and we've been put here to cram in as much knowledge and (more importantly) experience as we can handle. There may be no college courses in talent agentry, but there's nothing to stop you from developing your own curriculum. And you'll find that self-education is a lot cheaper and a lot more fun than four years at Harvard!

» *Read, Read, Read!*

In Appendix E I've included a bibliography of books you might want to purchase or borrow—and there are hundreds more being published every year! Check out your library, bookstores, and publishers lists from *Billboard* and *Variety*. Seek out books on marketing, sales, promotion, the myriad kinds of performing arts (music, dance, magic, hypnotism, clowning, mime, sideshow, circus, ventriloquism, vaudeville, theater, comedy, etc.), entrepreneurship, small business management, legal issues (contract law, for example), and foreign commerce.

And most important, to keep up on what's happening in entertainment, make it a habit to peruse the national show business periodicals—*Variety, BillBoard Magazine*, and *Agent & Manager*. As I point out later, they're not only a part of your "continuing education", but they are also a valuable source of new acts and new clients.

» *Enroll for Enrichment*

There are many excellent courses around that can be extremely helpful in your new business venture. Check the catalogs of your local universities, community and junior colleges, adult education programs, music schools, etc. Find out if your area has a Clowns of America chapter, or a Society of American Magicians group (or any of a number of other professional organizations for the different arts), and consider becoming a member or at least attending their monthly meetings. Ask your local Chamber of Commerce, Junior Achievement, Advertising Association, Service Corps of Retired Executives (SCORE), and other groups if they offer courses or workshops.

Over the years, I've taken courses and workshops in law, hypnotism, the business of music, witchcraft, radio newscasting, alternative healing, advertising, clowning, marketing, and video production. And believe me, they're not like those boring courses you took back in high school or college—they're actually a lot of fun, and they're low cost as well!

Chapter 2
Talent, Talent, Who's Got the Talent?

In this Chapter:

To sell, you gotta have "product", and as a talent agent, your product is talent, performers, acts, whatever. When you've finished with this chapter, you'll know how to:

- **Decide** what kind of talent you're going to handle
- **Scout** for talent
- **Handle** contracts and commissions
- **Set** performance fees
- **Cope** with talent-related problems
- **Keep** your stable happy and content

Generalize or Specialize?

What kind of agency do you want to run? A purveyor of heavy-metal bands? A source of kiddie entertainment? A speaker's bureau? A core of old-time circus and vaudevillian acts?

Which flavor you choose will depend on your own tastes and background, the acts you think have the highest marketability, and other factors. In any case, before you can start searching for talent, you first have to know what you're looking for.

If you're interested in catering to society affairs and weddings, then you'll want to stock up on 3- to 8-piece ensembles and dance bands. On the other hand, if you're going after arts festivals or grade schools, you'll want the more "theatrical" arts such as mime, puppetry, storytelling, and folk music. Or, if you'll be concentrating on promoting shopping malls and other businesses, you'll want some really zany, crowd-drawing, attention-getting acts like organ grinders and monkeys, one-man bands, acrobats, clowns, and magicians. Maybe you'd like to set up a speakers' bureau and provide lecturers on a variety of intriguing topics.

However, these categories aren't as rigid as they may seem ... I've hired out magicians to arts festivals, and acrobats and clowns to colleges.

Most likely, you'll want to dabble in several markets, as opposed to having all your eggs in one basket. After all, you may very well be the only talent agent in town, and you don't want to have to pass up business just because you don't have a certain type of act.

My personal advice is: be prepared for anything. It doesn't cost you a cent to have as many performers as you can fit in your file cabinet. I have a cabinet that's jam-packed with acts—some may never hear from me, some may get a call once or twice a year, and some I book regularly. But ... if anyone ever asks me for a tightrope-walking belly dancer, I know where to find one. And it doesn't cost the performers for you to add them to your roster.

Above all, do whatever you're most familiar with, and have the greatest amount of interest in, because that's what you're likely to be good at. As one wise sage put it, "Work at what you enjoy, and the rest will follow."

A Typical Stable of Talent

The best example I can give you of the variety of acts you can represent, is to list my own lineup. "Variety is the spice of life" they say, and this list certainly exudes "variety". It's important that you study this list. Take particular notice of the different categories and the number of acts in each category, because these constitute a good general mix.

Please note: This is a listing from the peak era of my agency, and many of these acts are no longer performing (sadly, some have passed over to the Great Stage in the Sky). Of those who are still active, you're welcome to book them yourself...few have 'exclusive agency' with anyone, including me. Of course if you live in western Montana, there's a little matter of distance and travel expenses, but rest assured, you'll find most of these kinds of acts in any state or country in which you happen to reside.

» *Animals, Petting Zoos, Rides*

- **Golden Ark Animal Attractions**. Petting zoo of over 50 domestic and exotic animals, plus pony and camel rides.
- **Commerford & Sons.** Popular petting zoo, and elephant, camel, and pony rides.
- **Al & Joyce Vidbell.** Assorted chimps, elephants, and other exotic creatures for performances and exhibition.

» *Caricaturists*

- **Jack Drummey.** The famed "Drum" of the Boston press sketches members of the audience and/or presents his popular "easel" show.
- **Mike Moriarity.** Experienced advertising, promotional, and sports cartoonist will draw your guests at lightning speed.

» *Children's Diversions*

- **The Fiddler & Dancing Bear.** Gypsy fiddler and large friendly (costumed) bear dance and play for children of all ages.
- **Grumbling Gryphons.** A multi-faceted children's theater presenting folktales and legends from around the world.
- **Magical Melodies with Wendy Frank** Puppetry, sing-alongs, storytelling, musical improvisation, and games.

- **Phyllis Campana.** Face Painter and Balloon Animals
- **Mystic Paper Beasts.** "Magic fairy tales, surrealistic dreams, puppet figures of whimsical charm mix with human actors in fanciful masks" *New York Times*

Figure 1. Fiddler & Dancing Bear Act

- **Uncle Fun.** Juggling, unicycling, accordion playing, acrobatics, and turn-of-the-century "big wheel" bicycling.

» Clowns and Circuses

- **Bertolino Bros. European Circus.** A cavalcade of acts under the Big Top, with star performers from all over Europe.
- **Bounce the Clown & Mademoiselle Ooo La La's Vaudeville Circus.** Juggling, equilibristics, unicycling, mime, music, and comedy in a 2-person, 3-ring circus.
- **Hilary Chaplain**, a.k.a. Celery Trashcan. Juggler, fire-eater, stiltwalker, clown, mime.
- **Cheezo the Clown.** Magic, balloon animals, robots, clownmobile, and stage.
- **Cabert Michaels.** Clowning, magic, and juggling, with Class.

Figure 2. The Late Capt. Don Leslie, Sideshow Man

- **Capt. Don, Swordswallower, Fire-eater, and Completely Tattooed Man.** A veteran of the old-time tent circus sideshows, now deceased. All unbelievably genuine.
- **Doc Swan's Circus Sideshow.** It's a big 10-in-1: the fire-eater, rubber girl, magician, juggler, Ms Electra, and all the rest.
- **Lula. Stiltwalking**, acrobatics, slackrope-walking, clowning-around, topsy-turvy juggling, and other entrancing skills.
- **Pif the Magic Clown.** Great for kids, with magic, balloon animals, streamers, games, and fun.
- **The Royal Palace Circus.** A circus package formed by two world-renowned circus families from Hungary and Italy, complete with spotted leopards, dogs, chimps, acrobats, clowns, and aerialists.
- **Silky the Clown.** The master of circus buffoonery, balloonery, jokes, and giant props.

» *Dramatists and Storytellers*

- **Judith Black.** Described by *The Boston Globe* as "a master storyteller in the Boston area, (who) has been a pioneer in the educational movement to bring storytelling into the classroom."
- **Brother Blue.** The balloon/ribbon/ spangled storyteller of the streets, now deceased.

- **On Tour…with Mark Twain and Oscar Wilde.** Two one-man shows that capture the essence of these legendary masters.

Figure 3. Duncan Inches as William Shakespeare

- **Shakespeare on Shakespeare.** "A Little Touch of William in the Night, with Duncan Inches", a one-man presentation that recreates Shakespeare's life, using as the basis "The Seven Ages of Man" and tracing the Bard from young manhood to old age. "Rivals Holbrook's Mark Twain in riveting its audience".
- **The Vision of Black Elk.** True stories of an Oglala Holy Man, as rendered dramatically by Manitonquat (Medicine Story).
- **Jerry Vovscko.** "Master storyteller, musician, Pied Piper, and child all rolled into one." Host of "The Discovery Store" on Channel 10 in Worcester.
- **West of the Moon.** Traditional stories from Africa, China, and America, with folksongs and limberjacks.

» *Music: Ethnic, Traditional, Classic, & Novelty*

- **Back Bay Brass Quintet.** Renaissance, baroque, romantic, impressionistic, and contemporary music.
- **Bagpipers and Bagpipe Bands.** Several to choose from, of various traditions.
- **Baroque and Bach by The Quartet.** Elegant 18th century music, light or sober.
- **Boogaloo Swamis**. Footstomping, crowd-pleasing Cajun music at its best.
- **Tom Callinan.** 20th Century Troubadour folksinger, sea chantyman, instrumentalist (14 at last count), and whaling historian and conservationist.
- **Chuck Morris and the Sidewalk Blues Band**. Traditional Chicago and Texas-style Blues.
- **Doug Ecker.** Traditional Irish dance and Renaissance music on hammered dulcimer, mandolin, violin, and bells.
- **Captain Fiddle** (Ryan Thompson). Probably one of the best known fiddle players in New England.

- **Flamenco al Aire Libre.** Raw flamenco dancing and music, played with a touch of the gypsy.
- **Herb Reed and the Platters.** Well-known group from the 50s and 60s.
- **Vera Meyer's Glass Harmonica.** Vera Meyer, concert performer and street musician, is one of only three glass harmonica players in the world today!
- **The Gloucester Hornpipe & Clog Society.** Original and traditional Irish and English jigs and reels; English, Irish, and early American songs and shanties, and folk dance music and instruction from around the world.
- **Irish Bands:** Devilish Merry, Bodger's Mate, Starboard List, Clamjamfree
- **Koli.** Fresh, energetic performance of traditional Yiddish, contemporary Hebrew, and familiar American showtunes and folk music.
- **Lorraine Lee and Bennett Hammond.** Virtuoso guitarist and Appalachian dulcimer master play traditional music of Europe and America.
- **The Linmax Nightlife.** The favorite duo-with -Big-Band-sound around the lounge circuit, playing all the contemporary hits.
- **National Jewish Music Ensemble.** Klezmer music for all occasions
- **The New England Song and Daunce Companie.** A complete Elizabethan feast, served by colorful characters dressed in authentic period costumes and speaking in English dialect, along with performances of songs, dances, and music of 17th century English country folk.
- **Paula's Famous German Band.** A group of six rollicking, boisterous Alpinites complete with lederhosen and omp-pah horns.
- **Bill Payne's Boston Jazz Band.** Good time music for any occasion, from Dixieland swing to contemporary jazz.
- **Tapestry. Renaissance**, Medieval, and traditional music on recorders, flutes, tin whistles, gothic harp, fiddle, guitar, bagpipes, percussion, and voice.
- **Third World Bands**: Metro Steel Orchestra, Jah Spirit, Volo Volo, Mariachi Guadalajara, Carribean Express, Mocha Java, Calypso Hurricane.
- **The Tuxedos.** Songs from the Big Band era plus contemporary; Bossa Nova, Swing tunes, old favorites.

» *Hypnotists*

- **Guy Anthony.** Master Hypnotist and billed as the World's Fastest, he'll have your audience in a trance before they know it.
- **Bob Joyce.** Demonstrations of the art and science of hypnotism, plus audience participation.

» *Impressionists*

- **Dick Coffin.** Man of 1,000 Voices and Faces Special "muppet", children's, and senior citizen's shows available.

» *Jugglers and Jesters*

- **Alexander's Follies.** A wild-and-crazy Court Jester who thrills audiences with his unicycling, juggling, and comedy.

- **The Amazing Larry Vee.** The "Master of Outlandish Tricks" offers juggling, fire-eating, fire juggling, and unicycle piggyback rides.
- **Obaz.** One of the weirdest, daringest, most colorful juggling acts you've ever seen. This international favorite, a graduate of the Hungarian School of the Arts, whirls knives, hoops, clubs, and fire torches to pulsating music, while outfitted in costume and mask that rivals KISS.
- **Ken Sherbourne.** Veteran juggler, star of "The Milton Berle Show", and associate of Tony Bennett, Red Buttons, Rowan & Martin, and Tiny Tim.
- **Tobi Benay.** Cigar box, ball, torch and club juggling, plus slackrope walking and chin & nose balancing.

» *Magicians and Mentalists*

- **The Magic of Christopher Robin.** Live animals, illusions, balloon animals, facepainting.
- **Dario and Company.** Magic, music, juggling, and illusions for the whole family.
- **Magic by George.** George Sateriale, recent guest with Tony Randall in Broadway's "International Stars of Magic Show".
- **Scalzo and Company.** "The Magician's Magician" Star of Radio City Music Hall, Broadway, the Mike Douglas Show, and the Topsfield Fair. *People Magazine* said "Scalzo and Company surely was the class act of the evening".
- **Peter Sosna's Magic** A delightfully funny magician who will keep you laughing as you thrill to his closeup magic and large-scale stage illusions.
- **Jon Stetson.** Direct to you from the White House where he's performed at children's parties, and several of the premier cruise lines where he's entertained adult audiences for many seasons.
- **The Mime and Magic of Jim Vetter** A unique blend of mime and magic that creates an exciting fantasy world filled with amazing magical characters. "He's terrific!" *Boston Museum of Science*

» *Mimes*

- **Trent and Melody Arterberry.** One of the most professional and respected mime teams in New England.
- **Celebration Mime Theater.** Theater of innovative interpretation.
- **Kitchensink Mime.** Featuring family and children programs that synthesize a variety of mime styles, such as "In Concert" and "Dreams on a String".
- **Gary Krinsky.** "Can't rave enough about Gary" said one client. A unique weaving of mime and poetic narrative, combined with music, storytelling, and juggling.
- **Royal Sorrel Jr.** French mime, street clown, jester, silent magician, and marvelous machinations.

» *Puppets, Marionettes, and Ventriloquists*

- **Bennington Puppets.** A touring marionette theater offering a half dozen productions to choose from.

- **Gary Brodeur & Co., Ventriloquist.** Great family and adult entertainment, with his sidekicks Rusty, Ralph, et al.
- **Dan Butterworth and His Marionettes.**
- **The Catskill Puppet People.** Marionettes, rod puppets, and life-sized puppets dramatize original tales for all ages.

Figure 4. Donna Marie and Friends

- **Donna Marie and Friends.** Meet Denny, Dachary, Merlin, Rackery, and Zackery; Western theme and facepainting also available.
- **John Tierny/Trees Are Terrific.** Environmental puppetry, with tree impersonations, animal puppet theater, and sign-language stories.
- Plus: Over 30 puppeteers associated with the Boston Area Guild of Puppetry, such as Gerwick Puppets, Poobley Greegy Puppet Theater, Starbird, Northeast Kingdom Puppets.

» *Speakers' Bureau*

- **Betty Hill.** The first UFO abductee, star of the book "Interrupted Journey" and the TV movie, "UFO Incident". (Now deceased.)
- **Art Meyers.** Best selling author ("The Ghostly Register", "Ghosts of the Rich and Famous", and "Ghosthunters' Guide") and noted authority on haunted houses and psychic phenomena. (Now deceased.)
- **Wicca: The Old Religion.** High Priests and Priestesses and various other leaders of Neopaganism and witchcraft talk about this sweeping New Age movement.

Figure 5. Ed and Lorraine Warren, Demonologists

- **Ed and Lorraine Warren, America's Demonologists.** Real-life ghosthunters and exorcists, and investigators of the Amityville Horror and other haunted houses. Ed has passed on, but Lorraine is still touring, lecturing, and investigating. Plus you can see Lorraine on A&E's *Paranormal State*.

» *Street Entertainers*

- **Stephen Baird, "Boston's #1 Streetsinger".** A rousing performance featuring his 6- and 12-string guitars, mandolin, dulcimer, banjo, autoharp, kazoos, tambourines, puppets, and loads of audience participation. For children of all ages.
- **Peter O'Malley.** Singer, magician, juggler, and comedian on skates.
- **The Original Hurdy-Gurdy Man.** Performs in the tradition of the medieval minstrel, combining music and theater to entertain both young and old. Features the hurdy-gurdy, crumhorn, pipe and tabor, and bowed psaltery. A shadow puppet show is also available.

Figure 6. RuthAnna, Streetsinger of Boston

- **RuthAnna, Street Minstrel, Concert and Recording Artist, and Songwriter.** "One of the best of many … her especial ease with her audience, and her skill with the recorder, autoharp, and guitar has made her one of the best acts … a truly DISTINCTIVE personality."

» *Vaudeville and Novelty Acts*

- **Jonathan Kalonymus Briskin.** When he's not being Dr. Briskin, Kalonymus performs Death-defying acrobatic feats, stilt walking, slack-rope walking, ladder balancing, unicycling, and juggling.
- **Heart of Gold Vaudeville Company.** Old-time sawdust vaudeville, with musical sawing, magic, juggling, shadowography, storytelling, stiltwalking, and more!
- **Royal Sorell, Jr., Mr. Balloon Man** – Master of balloon creations, and founder of the largest balloon art organizations in the country.
- **Goowin's Balloowins.** Madcap balloon artist Allynn Gooen creates instant balloon sculptures on children, dressing them as butterflies, dragons, and spaceships, and turning them into characters in zany theatrical tales.

- **Annie Hickman's All-American Bug Show.** A combination of costuming, puppeteering, miming, and dancing creates fantastic illusions of creatures from the insect kingdom.
- **Sgt. Pepperoni, World's Record One-Man Band.** A walking, marching, playing one-man band outfitted with over 26 different instruments, 12 of which he plays simultaneously.
- **Mr. Slim and L.J. Newton's Old-Time Vaudeville Revival.** A husband-and-wife team who are Maestros at juggling, banjo picking, comedy, and dance, and other assorted vaudevillean skills.
- **Leonard Solomon's Good-time Music and Vaudeville Review.** Featuring the Majestic Bellowphone A virtual one-man band, with a never-before-seen musical invention consisting of corrugated pipes, beach balls, cow bells, kazoos, reeds, horns, blocks, and other miscellaneous contrivances upon which are played classical, marching, and popular tunes, interspersed with comedic juggling.

» *Old West*

- **Barbara Autry and Joslyn.** Part of the famed Autry Family, stars of the Calgary Fair and fairs and rodeos across the country, bring you rope-twirling and lassoing magic that will fascinate and amaze you. Barbara has been promoted to the Great Corral in the Sky, but I believe Joslyn is still carrying on the family tradition.

» *And So Much More...*

And, in addition, we have nationwide connections to hundreds of other star performers, celebrities, musicians and bands of every conceivable style, carnivals and circuses, folk artists, and anyone and anything else you can imagine.

Can you find people in your town to fill every one of these slots? Probably not. But then again, you probably don't need a fire-eating sword-swallower or a dozen different clowns.

Talent Scouting

But, you ask, "How can I find talent in the backwater town I live in?" Fear not, because even in the farthest outreaches, there are hundreds of places you can prospect for talent.

» *14 Places to Find Talent No Matter Where You Live*

No matter what area of the country you live in, you can find talent under almost any rock. And here are some rocks to look under:

- Yellow Pages phone books
- Local coffeehouses
- Newspaper "calendar" listings
- Classified ads
- Club listings
- Community theaters
- Professional organizations

- Arts directories
- Student activities offices at colleges and schools
- Festivals, crafts shows, and fairs
- On the street
- TV and radio stations
- Other agencies (not only talent agencies, but modeling and acting agencies as well)
- *Cavalcade of Acts and Attractions,* and dozens of other show business directories (see Appendix E for a partial listing)

» *Evaluating Talent*

Once you've found them, how do you know who's good and who's not? If you're in touch with what's current, have an ear for music, and a sense of what's appealing, exciting, and satisfying, you'll know. That's one reason for sticking with the kinds of entertainment you're most familiar with. For example, if you're a folk music enthusiast, you'll have an idea of what constitutes good folk music.

But for those acts that fall outside your field of expertise, you'll have to rely on other people's judgment:

- Attend their performances,. watch the audience's reaction, and try to talk to some of the attendees after the show.
- Ask friends and associates who know something about the particular specialty (consider taking them along with you if you're going to audition a performer).
- Read any reviews or other press clippings the person might have but treat those puff pieces with a good dose of skepticism. There are all sorts of reasons why someone might write a rave review (maybe the reviewer is a relative or friend, maybe he or she has the hots for the performer, or just maybe the reviewer has abysmal taste).

» *4 Easy Steps in Approaching a Performer*

When you find someone you think is good, wait for an opening, walk right up to them, introduce yourself, and tell them you run a small talent agency (here's where you hand them your business card), that you enjoyed their work, and that you'd like to add them to your roster. Do this *after* the performance, if that's how you met them. Not only would they resent being interrupted during a performance, but if the performance has gone well, they'll be in a mellow mood and much more approachable than normally. At least one of my acts has complained that people have tried to storm the stage during a set just to ask for a brochure.

If they're the least bit hesitant, quickly point out that they can't lose by signing up with you. You're not going to put them under any exclusive contract, you'll try your best to get their asking price, and they'll always be free to accept or turn down any job you offer to them. Explain that their only obligation is to pay you your modest commission on any job they do accept.

If you're doing booking only on a parttime basis, be truthful and admit that your contribution to their career will be more of a supplemental nature than anything else. Don't lead them to expect more from you than you can honestly hope to deliver.

Get their full name, address, and phone number, and ask them to send you their promo package, which may consist of brochures, head shots, news clippings, and perhaps even an audio or video tape. Again, give them one of your business cards so they'll have your address and phone number.

Don't be hesitant or shy. Performers are happy to know that you enjoyed their act and were impressed enough to want to represent them. Many performers, particularly so-called street entertainers and those just starting out, have never attracted the attentions of an honest-to-god agent before, and will find the idea of "being represented" very appealing.

Once you and the performer have agreed to work together, the first step is to make sure you know everything you need to know about them, and for that I use a Performer Information Form (PIF), which you'll find in Appendix B.

» *Other Agents*

Sometimes you'll find that a performer is already listed with one or more agencies. This shouldn't present a problem, as rarely do such agencies have the performer under exclusive contract.

But even if they have an exclusive, you will usually be able to book the act through the other agency (you'll have to split the commission of course, but half a loaf is better than none, right?).

» *4 Important "Scouting" Reminders*

Here are a few things to keep in mind when "talent scouting" First impressions are important and you don't want to come across as a dolt.

- Be sure to get the spelling of their name (both their stage name and legal name) correct. For a while, I'd listed the "New English Song and Daunce Companie" in my promotional handouts as "The New England Song and Dance Company", and "PIF the Clown" as "PIS the Clown". Performers are even more sensitive about their professional names than you or I, so handle with care.
- Double check to make sure you have the correct fee for each type of performance. An act may do a roving performance or "walk around" for one fee, but charge a much higher price for a formal stage show. You'll be terribly embarrassed if you quote a client the "walk around" price for a stage show, and after discovering your mistake, be forced to go back to the client with the higher figure.
- Make certain you know the performer's limitations and conditions. For instance, some acts have too much equipment to do "walk arounds" or think that roving is beneath them and won't do them for any amount of money. Other acts can't perform in the open if it's windy or noisy. So don't propose an act for a situation they're not suited for.
- Be familiar with every act you book. Catch at least one performance so you can describe accurately what they do. And then try to catch their show once a year (or even more often if possible). You'd be surprised how much an act can change in content, format, quality, and personnel from one season to the next.

» *What About Booking Acts You Haven't Auditioned?*

Despite what I just said, there'll come a time when you have to fill an order with an act you've only heard or read about, but have never seen in person. It may be a last-minute situation, you may have no-one on your roster to fit the bill, or perhaps your one-and-only stilt walker is on the injured list or is already booked on that particular day. Whatever the reason, you're faced with the question, do you risk booking an unknown or don't you?

If you've heard of an act through relatively reliable sources (e.g., performers you've known for a while and whose judgment and integrity you respect, recognized arts directories or other listings, acts that have appeared at "name" venues, etc.), you can feel fairly safe in using them. However, just to be extra cautious, ask them for references when you call them to find out their fee and availability.

Handshakes and Contracts

OK, you've found an act. Where do you go from here? Before you dream of signing an *exclusive* contract, remember that, until you're experienced and have a sterling track record and are prepared to make this a full-time effort and concentrate on promoting a select few, you have no right to sign any act to an exclusive contract (or any other kind, for that matter). Until you reach the Big Time, be content with just a friendly handshake agreement between you and the performer.

» *Filling Out the Performer Information Form (PIF)*

What you should be focusing on is gaining an understanding of the act so you can sell them properly. And the first step is to capture all the information you'll need to know about them.

Be sure to have each new act fill out a PIF—Performer Information Form (see Appendix B). – not to be confused with Pif the Clown. And don't forget to update it each year—an act may change its format or personnel, raise its rates, etc. Then file away these sheets for quick reference.

Basically, the stuff you'll need to know includes:

» *Name of the act*

The stage name under which the act performs. See the caveat under "4 Important 'Scouting' Reminders" about the importance of getting this name right. You'll also need the names of the individual performers, for publicity, making out checks (if the group doesn't have a bank account in its name), and other reasons.

» *Contact's name*

The contact person for the act (generally relevant only if the act is a band or other group, or has a manager).

» *Mailing address*

The address to which all contracts, checks, etc. should be mailed.

» *Telephone number(s)*

Get more than one! Entertainers tend to move around a lot, and you want to be able to track them down, even if you haven't talked to them for a year or more. Get their cellphone number, home phone number, work number, and the phone number of any manager or answering service they may employ or that of a close friend. I've had to trace acts I've been out of contact with for three or four years, and believe me, it's a challenge if you have only a disconnected phone to work with.

» *Internet information*

Get their email address, website URLs, and anything else that'll be of use.

» *General availability*

Some performers are parttimers and have another job, so you'll want to know exactly when they're available. Also, you'll want to know about other obligations, how long they're willing to be away from home, if they'll work on holidays, etc.

» *Types of offerings*

Acts come in many shapes and sizes. Some acts will work outdoors, some will do roving performances, some will only do stage shows. Some acts (such as jugglers and mimes) offer workshops on their particular skills, either alone or as a follow-up to their act. Some preface their performance with a "teaser"—a brief sampling of their performance designed to draw the crowds in (much like the teasers you see at sideshows and strip shows).

» *Fees*

This should be set up as a matrix, covering the pricing scale for the various types of performances, the sizes of audiences, the classes of clients, block booking (multiple performances at one site or in one region). The Performer Information Form provides columns for these different situations, and to record any discounts they may offer to non-profit institutions and charitable events.

» *Funding*

Is the performer subsidized by organizations such as the National Endowment for the Arts? There are many groups that will subsidize the fees of approved acts when they perform at schools, libraries, and museums.

» *Additional charges*

What about additional monies for mileage, food, lodging, and other long distance travel expenses?

» *Requirements*

This covers performance space, staging, sound systems, lighting, props, and other things that the act has requested. What do they bring with them, and what do they need the client to supply? Be sure to write these in the "Riders and Additional Provisions" section when filling out the contract.

» *Contractual obligations*

Some acts may be signed up with other agents, either on an exclusive or non-exclusive basis. Usually this presents no major problem, as most agents are glad to cooperate for a split of the

Tom "Wolf" Elliott

commissions. However, make sure you know with which agents an act has signed, whether they're exclusive (and in what market areas), or non-exclusive, and on what basis they'll work with other agents. An example: one of my acts is signed with an agent who has exclusive rights to book that act into colleges. If I get that act a job at a high school, there's no obligation, but if I obtain an engagement at a college, I would first have to check with that agent for approval and reach an agreement on the commission.

» *Social security number*

Some contracts, such as those from state institutions, large businesses, etc., require the performer's SS# for IRS purposes, so you might as well get it now so you'll have it when you need it later. Also, if the fees pass through your agency rather than being paid directly to the performer, you'll have to issue a 1099 at the end of the year if you've written checks over a certain amount for the year, and you'll need the SS# for that.

You can never have too much information about anything, so get it while you have the opportunity.

Commissions

It goes without saying that commissions represent the biggest source of your income, so it's important to set a rate that's going to cover your expenses and leave a margin for profit, and yet be competitive. Commission rates vary widely—I've heard of some as low as 10%, and others as high as 25-30%. I started out with 10%, found it was too low, so now am currently charging 15%, which seems to work for me.

By the way, commissions are calculated on the performance fee only; all additional payments for such expenses as lodging, food, and travel go to the performer.

» *2 Ways to Calculate Commissions*

There are two ways to calculate commissions. One way is to book an act at its standard fee, then deduct your commission from it and pay the performer the balance. The other way is to find out what the performer wants to "clear" and then add your commission on top of it before quoting a price. If you choose the former, you can truthfully tell your clients that they're paying no more to book the act through you than they would if they'd booked it direct. In the case of the latter, it doesn't cost the act anything to get a booking through you.

If I had to recommend one approach over the other, I'd probably argue that since you're working for the performers, they should be the ones who bear the cost. Also, this ensures that the price I quote is the same as the price the clients would be quoted if they'd contacted the act directly. And, if a prospect should say, "Sorry, I don't work through agents because I don't want to pay a surcharge (commission)," I can truthfully tell then that they're not paying the commission, the performer is. And then I point out that they're getting my expertise and services for free! How can they lose?

But what about the performer? How do they feel about *my* commission coming out of *their* pockets? Generally, they're happy to pay me my fee (well, maybe "happy" is an overstatement, but they certainly don't protest), because any job I find for them is a job they probably wouldn't have stumbled across on their own, and a date that would have probably otherwise gone unfilled.

So, the performer benefits by keeping busy, the client benefits by getting my services at no cost, and I benefit by collecting my commission. A class win-win situation!

Again, that doesn't mean you can't work it the other way, too. If you decide to tack the commission onto the regular fee, you can justify it on the basis that the client should pay for your services because it saves them a lot of booking headaches.

» *Collecting Commissions*

Don't worry about collecting your commissions. As I've said before, I don't have a formal agreement with my performers about getting paid, and you shouldn't really need one. Why? Because they know if they welch on a commission, they won't be getting any more jobs from you, and jobs are their lifeline.

However, you may want to give each of your acts a short, printed summary of how you operate just so there'll be no misunderstandings: whether you'll be signing contracts as their legal representative, to whom the checks are made out, how and when commissions are paid, how return engagements are contracted, etc.

» *Commissions on Return Engagements*

That last point—return engagements—is extremely crucial to your financial success. Once you've gotten an act into a venue, any return engagements must be booked through you for the usual commission, even if the purchaser contacts the performer directly. Repeat business is where you make your real money. If you don't have an exclusive contract with your performer, you can easily be cut out of the deal, so you have to rely on the honesty and ethics of both the client and the performer. And the best way to do that is to make sure everyone understands how the game is played …

Setting Fees

What an act charges–that is, their fee schedule–is, of course, solely up to the act. And they have the final decision on each and every offer, not you! Just like a real estate agent, you're legally and morally obligated to pass on every offer to the performer and let him or her decide whether or not to accept it. So I make sure I give an act the chance to accept or reject every job, no matter how low the fee offered..

I usually keep two fee schedules in my head—one is the standard fees, the other is the absolute minimum an act will accept. That way, I know within what limits I must negotiate.

» *Variables Affecting Fees*

Prices vary not only from performer to performer, but also on the type of performance wanted. A full stage show almost always costs more than an informal mini concert or "walk-around". A one-hour performance costs more than a half-hour (but usually not twice as much, because travel time, set-up time, and preparation time are the same for both), and discounts are usually given for multiple shows in the same day. Prices also vary according to the season, the day of the week, and the time of day—after all, prime time is prime time. For bands, weekends are prime time, but they may be willing to take a Tuesday night gig for a reduced fee.

Don't always believe what you might see on a performer's fee schedule—of such stuff are dreams made. I've known acts who never once came close to actually getting the prices printed on their brochure. You have to be practical about pricing and encourage your performers to be likewise. Pretending that such inflated prices are realistic hurts both of you. Sure, you might occasionally encounter a naive client who'll fall for an exorbitant price, but word eventually gets around when an act is overpricing themselves.

And don't buy the philosophy that high prices command "respect"—an act's true worth and the respect it's due will be evident in the first five minutes they're on stage.

As one of my acts put it, "A high price does not always command respect". But a price somewhat above the budget walk-around benefits certain types of acts. When a client pays a premium price for an act, generally that client will go the extra mile in making sure that all conditions are met to ensure a good show. A client may regard a $75 clown as a "throw away", but they'll make sure that a $1000 act is treated and presented in the best way possible.

» *Travel Expenses*

Also, don't forget to add travel, lodging, and other expenses when you're quoting prices, especially for remote engagements (over 25 miles away from the performer's home base). Unless an act has put down specific charges for these items on the Performer Information Form, use the standard IRS allowance for mileage if the performer is driving there, otherwise use actual costs (plane fares, etc.). If lodging will be needed and the act agrees to this, give the client the option of providing it or reimbursing the performer at cost. Some performers are happy to be put up in someone's guest room or even on the living room sofa, while others insist on a motel or hotel room. Institutions such as colleges and large companies may have on-site dorms or a corporate room at a nearby hotel.

» *Some Typical Fee Schedules*

Occasionally, a new act won't have a fee schedule and may ask you for advice. Because of the varying economic conditions throughout the country and the fluctuations over the past decade, I can't give you a hard-and-fast guide, but I *can* tell you the price ranges I'm currently working with (in 2008) in the New England area (one of the higher cost regions of the US):

- *Bands*
  Standard performance is two 45-minute sets, at $200/person for 6- to 8-piece bands, and $250/person for smaller ensembles. The minimum price for any band is at least $600.

- *Folksingers and other solo musicians*
  $200-400 for two 45-minute sets on stage. $100-200/hour for roving musicians, minstrels, and troubadours.

- *Magicians*
  $500-1,000 for a full-scale stage show with large illusions. Simple walk-arounds featuring close-up magic go for $125-175/hour.

- *Mimes, clowns ,jugglers*
  $200-$350 for a formal, one-hour stage show. $100-175/hour (or $300-500/day) for walk-arounds. $100-175 for birthday parties and other small private affairs.

- *Novelty Acts (One-man bands, vaudeville shows, swordswallowers, acrobats)*
  $250-$400/performance. These acts, by their nature, are relatively short (20 to 30 minutes per set), but what they lack in length, they sometimes make up in thrills and, in some cases, danger.

- *Puppet shows*
  $150-$300 for most hand puppet shows. Some marionette shows, because of the complex staging needed, go for $600-1000 and more.

- *Theater troupes*
  Varies greatly according to size of troupe and complexity of production. Children's theaters usually get $500-800. Adult theater programs, such as "An Evening with Shakespeare", get $1,000-2,000 and even more.

- *Speakers*
  $250-700, unless they're really celebrity level.

- *Ventriloquists and hypnotists*
  Minimum of $300 for a 45-minute stage show, $350-750 for some of the better-known acts.

» *Feeling Comfortable about Fees*

One final point concerning fees: don't take on acts that ask fees you don't feel comfortable with (especially if they're inflexible).

What are some of the reasons you might feel uncomfortable? You may feel the act has blatantly overpriced itself. Or the fee may be way above the budget limits of your average client. (Champagne prices and beer budgets don't mix well.) Maybe you just lack confidence, or the act may simply be out of your league. For these and other reasons, bypass such acts for the time being. You can always pick them up later.

During my early years, I just wasn't confident asking for more than $200, so I passed up a number of acts that were asking more. Some of these acts are still around and presumably raking in even higher fees, others have dropped out of sight.

Remember—you can't sell something you don't honestly believe in—unless, of course, you're a born con artist, and that's the kind of talent agent we don't need.

Problems

Everybody has problems, and performers are no exception. If you stay in the business for any length of time, you'll encounter performers who are difficult, people who are not dependable, people battling booze or drugs.

You'll have acts that pull out at the last minute because they got a better offer. You'll have talent that will mouth off to somebody in the audience, or use foul language in a kiddies' show.

If a performer really screws up—a "no show", uncooperative, vulgar, or inebriated—most agents would advise you to drop him or her like the proverbial hot potato. You've invested too much in your own reputation to have it ruined by one bad apple.

As an object lesson, I recall the time I booked a series of acts for the summer season in Saratoga Springs in upstate New York. The very first performer I'd scheduled for the season lost his temper, started swearing at the audience, and came close to being forcibly removed from the stage. As a result, the client canceled all the other acts I'd booked there for the remainder of the summer. Not only was my reputation tarnished, but those other acts lost an opportunity and income as well. You want to bet I'll ever book that act again–anywhere?

I've talked to many another agents about this, and more than one has remarked about one of their problem performers, "He'll never work for me again!"

» *Performers and "Performance Rights"*

One particular problem you'll hopefully never encounter, but one you should educate your performers about, is the subject of performance rights.

I'm not going to try to give you a Law 101 course (however, taking a few courses on contracts and entertainment law might be advisable at some point), but I'll briefly describe the concept.

» *What are "performance rights"?*

Just as books are copyrighted, any performance (live, over the airwaves, recorded, etc.) of a copyrighted musical work is an infringement of that copyright unless a fee is paid to the copyright owner as compensation for the use of his or her creation. Under the present law, no one is exempt; even non-profit institutions and the smallest of coffeehouses are liable.

Does that mean that in order to sing or play someone's song you have to track that person down, negotiate a fair price, and pay them in the coin of the realm? No, clearly that would be virtually impossible. To avoid all that, performing rights associations have been set up to handle the collection and disbursement of these performance fees.

» *Performance rights associations*

ASCAP (American Society of Composers, Authors, and Publishers), BMI (Broadcast Music Incorporated), and SESAC are the largest of these associations. What happens is, the owner of the copyright (usually the songwriter) registers his or her song with one of these organizations, and that organization monitors the use of that song in clubs, lounges, and in coffeehouses, on radio and TV, etc.).

As it would be highly impractical for each performer to tally up how many times last month he or she sang a particular song (or for a club owner to do the same), most clubs, theaters, radio and TV stations, and other entertainment outlets have joined ASCAP, BMI, and SESAC and pay them a set license fee each month, based on such factors as number of seats, the price of admission, the market share, and so forth, and the resultant "kitty" is later divided among the copyright holders in proportion to the amount of play their songs received nationwide.

» *Infringements*

Infringements, unfortunately, are rife. How many small clubs, coffeehouses, or churches do you think belong to ASCAP? Most such infringements go unreported and unpunished, but there are severe penalties, at least on the books, to the tune of several hundred dollars for each infringement. And here's where you come in: if your performer is caught playing someone else's composition in an unlicensed place (one that has not paid a license fee to the appropriate performing rights organization), the performer and the owner of the establishment can both be held liable.

The shocking truth is that most fledgling performers haven't the foggiest notion about all this, and are therefore vulnerable. So make sure each of your musical acts understands the situation and their liability. Then, if they decide to go ahead anyway and take their chances, it will be a calculated risk and not an ignorant one.

If possible, encourage your performers to have a stash of original and "public domain" music in reserve for those occasions where they're not covered.

» *Unions*

Another legal problem you may encounter on occasion is unions. Just like certain professionals, laborers, and other workers, some actors, actresses, and other performers belong to organizations. Such membership usually dictates that they deal only with fellow members, both in terms of who represents them and by whom they are engaged. Thus (theoretically at least), a union performer can be represented only by a union agent, and can perform only in a union theater or concert hall, and only alongside other union performers.   And they must be paid at union scale. In some cases, certain exemptions apply (e.g., small theaters and non-profit institutions can sometimes get permission to pay an actor at less than union scale, or combine union and non-union actors in the same play).

The two largest theatrical unions are the American Federation of Television and Radio Artists (AFTRA) and the Screen Actors Guild (SAG). Frequently, a performer will belong to both organizations, as they are the key to getting work in the TV, radio, and movie industries. There are also unions for the many "industries" within the world of entertainment, from movie projectionists and lighting and audio technicians, to screenwriters and directors.

If you have any questions about their rules and regulations, I suggest you contact them directly. Most such organizations maintain offices in the top 10 US cities, and your local Yellow Pages will have a listing of the ones in your area.

5 Ways to Keep Your Stable Happy

Remember, your artists and performers are the second part of your profit formula, and if you don't have them, you have nothing to sell.

Recognizing their value, I've devised Five Commandments For keeping performers happy:

- Keep in contact with them.
- Respect their wishes and try to get them what they want.
- Represent them honestly, sell them enthusiastically, give them the detailed information they need, and pay them promptly.
- Compliment them and encourage them frequently.
- Keep them from starving.

The first two commandments are key, so I'll address each of them in greater detail below.

» *Keeping in Contact*

That first commandment is an important one! Performers thrive on attention and appreciation, so never neglect them. Even if no jobs come in for a while, be sure and keep in active contact to let them know you haven't forgotten them. I do this in several ways:

- Send them a PIF (Performer Information Form) every year or two, so they can change the information on file.
- Get a report. Call them after a job and ask them how things went. (This serves two purposes: not only am I demonstrating an interest in their welfare but, if there was some sort of problem, I'll be forewarned before I hear from the client.)
- Keep them updated. Send out an occasional newsletter, telling them about some of the jobs you've contracted recently, so they'll be aware that even though nothing's come through for them personally you're still alive and working.
- Remember them at the holidays. Mail them a card on Christmas and other special holidays like their birthday, if you know when it is.
- Chew the fat. Call them up every now and then just to chat and catch up on what's been happening with them. This is an excellent way to keep up on trends and get a general "reading" of what's going on in particular venues. Many times a performer will give me a tip about someone who's looking for a certain type of entertainment, or that a client is about to go bankrupt, or that an event has been canceled or postponed. My performers are also my friends, and I naturally treat them that way.

» *Getting Them What They Want*

And the second commandment is like unto it: Get them the money and treatment they expect. It's very important to get the performers what they've asked for in terms of fee, travel and lodging, maps, performance space, adequate setup and knockdown time, lighting, sound system, props, dressing room, and all the other details. Remember: a performer has enough to do to put on a good performance and shouldn't be expected to cope with unpleasant "surprises" and other hassles. That's your job, and one reason the performer is paying you a commission. And a good show, well received, makes everyone look good–performer, talent agent, and client.

Chapter 3
Finding Clients

In this Chapter:

Now that you have something to sell, you need someone to sell it *to*. The Client. The Marketplace. The Prospect.

You're likely very concerned about how, and where, and to whom you're going to market all these talented people you've "discovered". So when you've finished with this chapter, you'll know how to:

- Find potential customers.
- Manage your sales contacts
- Produce marketing collateral
- Use direct mail, telemarketing, advertising, public appearances, and other methods to increase sales.

3 Places to Look for Customers

Think it's going to be hard to find prospects in your corner of the world? Think again. We Americans are an active bunch, and you'll find that there are more prospects out there than you can reach in your lifetime. And they're growing all the time. Here are some places to look for prospects:

- Newspapers
- Directories
- Industry Source Books

» Read the Newspapers!

Just pick up your daily or weekly newspaper and skim over its weekly calendar of events, the engagement and wedding announcements, the society pages, church activities, and reports from civic clubs, lodges, and other social organizations. Almost every such item represents a potential job for one of your acts! If an event is still a ways off, call or write immediately. If it's too late to do anything this time around, make a note on your calendar to contact them in advance next year. And don't forget to check those freebie 'shoppers guides', as they too might alert you to promising opportunities.

There are more kinds of "news" than the one that gets tossed on your doorstep. Watch for posters and bulletin board notices advertising upcoming events. I've found this a particularly good source of new markets while traveling through the towns and hamlets in some of the farther reaches of my "territory". In doing so, I've come across fund-raisers, PTO shows, charity benefits, and other events.

» *Scan the Directories!*

Directories are big business these days, and you'll find that there's a ton of directories printed every year, based on every conceivable theme. Obtain directories and other compilations of local college and universities, secondary schools (public and private), fairs and festivals, nightclubs, coffeehouses, and other markets in which you have an interest. Also check your local yellow pages for lists of:

- Amusement and theme parks and other tourist attractions
- Charities and other non-profit institutions
- Churches
- Clubs (public and private)
- Colleges and schools (public and private)
- Function halls
- Hospitals
- Hotels
- Lodges
- Municipal Park & Recreation departments
- Museums
- Party supply outlets
- Restaurants
- Senior Citizen centers and nursing homes
- Shopping malls
- Stores

and any other place that may have an occasional need for entertainment.

And, if you have a computer and an Internet connection, you'll even find directories on-line if you can log on to the appropriate bulletin boards.

» *Check the Industry "Source Books"!*

Find out what arts directories, entertainment periodicals, business journals, and advertising newspapers are published in your area, and consider running an ad in one or more of them.

Scan a number of the national entertainment and advertising periodicals—*Agent & Manager, Billboard*, etc., and note any personnel changes reported there (e.g., "Charles Goodard

Appointed Special Events Coordinator for Six Flags Parks"), new ventures (e.g., "New Mexican Fast-Food Chain Debuts"), and who's currently booking (e.g., "2010 World's Fair Lining Up Attractions").

Check around for performing arts foundations, resource centers, and clearing houses—non-profit groups that help individuals and organizations plan events, including scouting up talent, and list your agency with them as a resource.

Consider joining the National Association for Campus Activities (NACA, an organization that provides a way to get into the college market and to showcase your lineup), your state and county fairs (which may provide an annual talent showcase), Chambers of Commerce, and other entertainment/business groups. As a member of these groups, you can usually obtain a membership list for prospecting.

Approach your "party needs" outlet, function facilities, social clubs, and restaurants, and see if you can work out some sort of deal where they put you in touch with their customers who are booking weddings, parties, and other social events.

List your agency in the national entertainment directories such as the *Cavalcade of Acts and Attractions*, and their specialized ancillary directories. Unlike years ago when these directories were in the form of thick books that quickly became outdated, many of them are now available online, making things easier for all concerned. Most listings are free, unless you want to create a very elaborate ad. See Appendix E for a listing of these magazines.

Also consider listing your agency in the Yellow Pages, city directories, shoppers' guides, and other local publications.

Setting Up a Contact File

Drawing from all of these sources of information, begin to build your Contact or Client Information Form (CIF) file. Ideally, if you've taken my advice about purchasing a computer, you'll store this file on there, but you can also use a recipe card file, or sheets in a 3-ring binder. Call each contact, and on a contact sheet (or in each record), include:

- The individual's name (and title, if any)
- The company or organization
- Address and phone number
- Name and title of any additional contacts
- Date(s) and brief description(s) of any events for which that person or organization might need entertainment.

For each event, also include:

- Budget(s)
- Special requirements
- Number and types of acts desired, and what they want each act to do
- Source of listing (newspaper, directory, inquiry, etc.)

Make sure that each record is large enough so that later you can enter a notation about each contact you've had with them and each act you've booked with them. You'll probably arrange your file alphabetically, by company or organization name, but you should also code each form with a number indicating the month in which they do their booking. That way, you can flip through the contact records each month and contact those clients or prospects who will be booking during that month. You'll find a sample Client Information Form in Appendix B.

» *When You Don't Know Whom to Ask for*

Any contact—by phone or mail—is much more effective if you have a name to ask for. But with new accounts, that's not always possible and you'll have to make an educated guess as to whom to ask for. Here are some common departments and titles:

- Colleges and Universities: Director of Student Activities (or Affairs)
- Secondary Schools: Principal, Headmaster, PTO President
- Fairs and Festivals: Chairperson, Festival (Fair) Committee
- Coffeehouses: Coffeehouse Manager
- Nightclubs and Restaurants: Manager

» *Keeping Your Contact File Updated*

I can't stress enough how important your contact file is, and how you must give top priority to keeping it up to date if you're to have a smoothly functioning, professional, and profitable agency. In the course of the year, you'll be:

- Making changes to personnel information, mailing addresses, and phone numbers
- Adding new prospects and new events
- Removing prospects who have disappeared from the scene or have not responded to repeated sales contacts. (In some cases, you'll find it's just not worth your time and money to keep some people on your mailing list; either place them on inactive status or remove them from the file entirely.)
- Recording engagements: the date, performer, fee, client satisfaction, and other details of each booking.

Your contact file is essential to every facet of your operation. Not only will you be using it for sales prospecting, but you'll need it to recall past transactions (like "What did the Wellington Shopping Mall pay for those two clowns last summer and how long did they work?"), for billing both clients and performers ("Who still hasn't paid me their commission?"), and for income tax reporting ("What are the total commissions I took in this year?").

Sales Literature

Now that you've got your prospect list, what do you do with it? Well, you could do a mailing. But first you have to have something to mail. And that's where your sales literature comes in—and you're going to need plenty of it. To use in direct mail campaigns, to hand out at trade shows and other events, and to send out in response to inquiries.

» *Designing a Printed Promo Piece*

How do you go about designing a mailing piece—let's say, a general brochure about your agency and its services?

If your talents don't happen to run along those lines and you have the money, you might want to hire a professional: someone who prepares sales literature for a living. But with a minimum of ability, you can take a shot at it all by yourself! And if you happen to have a computer with some desktop publishing software (or at least a word processor) installed and a printer attached, you can even print it yourself!

» *8 Tips for Designing a Promotional Piece*

Here are some simple steps to follow:

1. Decide on the purpose of the piece and what it should contain. Some pieces will summarize all the acts your agency offers. Other pieces will highlight individual performers, especially when you're doing seasonal mailings. And still others might give a profile of you and your agency.
2. Don't try to be too sophisticated or fancy, just be reasonably neat and professional.
3. Write in a clear, crisp style—lots of "punchy", short sentences. Leave a lot of white space—it'll make it look more upscale and readable.
4. Include quotes from satisfied customers, newspaper reviews of performances, and anything else that will inspire confidence in you and what you have to offer.
5. Don't include prices, or your address or phone number if you're planning on printing a huge quantity. If you're like most people, this kind of stuff changes too frequently, and preprinting such information on a piece is a sure way of making it outdated before its time. Instead, quote prices by the job, and stamp (or use stickers) for your address and phone. (Of course if you're using a computer to print a piece on an as-needed basis, you can put in this information and change it anytime.)
6. Make it visually attractive. Get the advice of someone with a good sense of layout and typography if you need to. If you're a do-it-yourselfer, dress up the piece with a photo, clip art (reproducible pen-and-ink illustrations that you can clip from books of such art, sold at art stores and through the mail for such purposes), borders, etc. Some of your acts may have sketches of themselves or eye-catching black-and-white photos they'd be happy to let you use.
7. Double-check your piece for accuracy and typos, and make sure you've included everything before you go to press.
8. Print no more than a month's supply. If you can't reproduce it on your computer, and don't have access to a good photocopy machine, take it to a copy center and have them print it on heavy stock (cover stock is one choice). Don't print too many, because I guarantee that you'll want to make changes to it as soon as it comes off the press. And there's nothing worse (or more wasteful) than having a 1,000 copies you have to get rid of before you can do a new version. Besides, since you probably have your own print shop with a computer and printer, you can print copies as you need them!

I've included a few samples in the Appendices.

» *3 Promo Pieces You Must Have*

At a minimum, you should plan to have:

- A general agency brochure, that tells what services you provide, the range of performers you handle, etc.
- Seasonal pieces, highlighting acts that are especially suited to special holidays and celebrations. I do ones for Spring, Summer Recreational Programs, Halloween, and The Holidays (Thanksgiving-Christmas-New Years)
- Pieces highlighting specific performers. Some of your performers might be able to supply you with their own literature (see below), or at least with the photos, reviews, and other things you'll need to produce your own.

» *8 More Goodies for Your Promo Package*

In addition to your general agency brochure, you should also have the following on hand:

- Advertising specialties
- Agency Newsletter
- Brochures supplied by your performers
- Business cards
- Client list
- Glossies
- News clippings
- Song lists (musical acts)

— *Advertising premiums and novelties*

I've used such gimmicks ("advertising specialties", they're called in the trade) as foreign coins, imprinted calendars, personalized pens and pencils, and other give-aways, tied somehow to the theme of the particular mailing, to give it that added punch. For example:

- An appropriate coin to illustrate the message, "Want to Save a Few Pence on Entertainment?"
- An imprinted wallet-sized calendar with the message, "Save Time, Money, and Hassles—Book Your Next Entertainment through (agency name)".
- An exotic, colorful foreign stamp for the theme, "This Stamp is like Our Line-up of Acts: RARE, EXOTIC, ATTENTION-GETTING!"

— *Agency newsletter*

Another popular item is a newsletter, emailed monthly or seasonally, and containing announcements of any changes, profiles of old and new acts, recent bookings, availabilities, upcoming tours, etc. This is an excellent vehicle for highlighting those new acts you've just signed on, and titillating your readers with anecdotes about some of your old acts. You can also use it to pat yourself on the back when you've enjoyed some particular success. I published such a newsletter for a period, and when I stopped, people actually called or wrote to tell me how much they missed it!

— Brochures and other materials supplied by your performers

Since many of your acts may already have their own brochures or 1-sheeters, ask them if they'll give you a supply to include with your mailings. If they're low on stock or are otherwise unwilling to provide literature in quantity, ask them if they'll give you a clean copy suitable for reproduction. Then take it down to your copy center or to a good photocopy machine, and run off a bunch of copies. Using your performer's literature will save you a substantial amount of money and provides you with materials that are probably more professional looking than you could afford on your own.

— Business cards

Be sure to include business cards with your mailings. They cost only pennies, and many of your clients maintain files of such cards to refer to when they need a product or service. VistaPrint is a wonderfully inexpensive source of business cards. Don't buy those cheap, "thermographed", one-style-fits-all white business cards you see advertised on matchbook covers and in the classifieds at the back of magazines. Instead, invest in some good, full-color cards printed on sturdy linen stock—they'll project a better impression, and that's worth every penny.

— Client lists

Include one sheet that lists the places where an act has appeared. Or, on the agency level, include a sheet listing all the clients you've worked for. Indicate those that have done repeat business with you, or have invited an act back again.

— Glossies (5x7 or 8x10 photographs)

Photos are another standard ingredient that can make a big impression, so try to include them in your mailings whenever you can. Also, your clients will frequently ask you for photos to use in their own publicity efforts, such as articles in the local newspaper. The same philosophy applies here: if a performer is willing to give you a supply, take them and use them. If not, ask for one copy, take it to a photo shop, and have them duplicate it. Black-and-white copies are surprisingly low cost these days, and you should be able to get 100 8x10s for under $100. Always stamp each photo with your name and address before mailing it out. People will hold on to a nice-looking picture long after they've misplaced the brochure or business card that accompanied it.

If you're going to be using a lot of photos, go to a lithographer and have the photo printed. And if you're going to be using the photo in your literature, have some pre-screened (sometimes called line shots) made so you don't have to pay for screening (breaking down the photo into those newspaper-type dots) every time you want to use it.

If an act has no suitable photo, it might be a good idea to have one taken, particularly if the act has a strong visual impact. You might do this on a co-op basis: you pay half and the act pays half. If you decide to go this route, try to find someone who's a semi-professional photographer—you don't necessarily need a Bachrach. Or check with the photographers at your hometown newspaper, who might be looking to make some spare change. Shoot both color and black and white (color's great, but who can afford to print the number of copies you'll need?). Have them printed as proof sheets, select the one or two best photos, and then have those enlarged and printed. 8x10 is the preferable size. Use a commercial photo finisher (one who does industrial and professional photo printing, and has the equipment to do it fast and cheap), not your corner drugstore.

— *Newspaper clippings*

If your act has been written up in a newspaper or other review, get a copy. Phone or write the editor of the publication for permission to reprint. Then photocopy the article and include it in your press kit. You might also want to do the same with other articles, like "The History of Old-time Vaudeville", "Halloween Mysteries", or "The Return of the Big Band Era", if such topics are pertinent to a mailing.

— *Song lists*

For bands and other musical acts, include a sheet listing their repertoire of musical selections, grouped by either category or artist.

» *The "Packaged" Look*

If you are planning to use several pieces together, or mail them separately in a series of mailing to the same list, give them some common corporate identity so they look like they came from the same place and belong together. Some suggestions for achieving a unified look include:

- Print the pieces on the same color and stock of paper.
- Add a logo (a symbol or unique typestyle)
- Use the same layout, typography, and style of illustrations.

If you do this right, people will begin to recognize your "signature" whenever they receive a mailing from you.

» *Keeping Your Package Current*

As your agency and your acts grow, make sure your promo kit grows with them. Every year or so, check over each act's materials and be sure to add any new bits of information, places where the act has performed, and new personnel.

Just like in the supermarket, if it's "New and Improved", be sure to let the public know!

Let the Postman Do the Walking: Using Direct Mail

Yes, I know, most business correspondence these days is over the Internet. But direct mail, particularly when you mail to a select list of proven buyers on a regular basis, can be an extremely powerful marketing approach. Think about it – you're still getting ads and other solicitations in the mail every day, aren't you? So it must be working, right? And once you've "massaged" and pruned your contact list for a year or two, you'll find that these periodic mailings (particularly at the time of year they hire their talent) can be tremendously effective.

Repeat business is your bread and butter, and makes the difference between success and failure. One-shot deals can be nice too, but depending on cultivating new sources of revenue all the time can be costly. The repeats are your return on the money and time you've invested in digging up new business in the past. Without repeats, your profit margin is going to be very small.

Another way to look at repeat business is that it's like the Golden Goose. Once clients have gotten in the habit of ordering from you, you can just sit back, pick up the phone when they call, arrange for what they want, and collect your commission—and it doesn't cost you a cent in additional marketing or advertising!

» *"Mass Mailings" vs "Individualized Mailings"*

Basically there are two kinds of direct mail: mass mailings, and individualized mailings. And both are relevant whether you're using 'snail mail' or email.

— *Mass mailings*

This refers to mailing the same exact package to a sizable number of people, e.g., everyone in your contact file, or every shopkeeper within a 10-mile radius, or every school in your part of the state, or to everyone is a particular business directory. Mass mailings are usually first-time mailings, although the term can apply to any large mailing. These can be done once a year, but I'd suggest doing them seasonally to rack up some holiday business. And don't forget to send seasons greetings around the holidays to everyone in your file. Things to include in a mass mailing:

- Your agency brochure, at least in the first mailing.
- A list of current clients, particularly those in the same category as the addressees (for example, I have one sheet for the "Fairs and Festivals" market, listing all of the fairs and festivals I've done business with).
- Business cards (be generous and include a couple; your contact may want to pass them around)
- Optionally: Glossies, sheets on individual acts, agency newsletter

— *Individualized mailings*

Individualized mailing is mailing a custom packet to specific individuals. This is a common approach when mailing a packet to someone around the time they usually do their bookings, or when you're promoting a particular act.

Such mailings almost always go to people with whom you've done business before, or with whom you've had some previous contact.

There are at least two items you should include in any individualized mailings:

- A sheet and/or glossy on the act(s) you want to promote
- A letter explaining why you're mailing this packet to them at this particular moment or why you're recommending this act. For example, "Over the past year, they've played to sell-out crowds at the Pablo County Fair, the Arkansas Cornhuskers Festival, the Eastern States Exposition, and other fairs just like yours" or "The Burpee Bros., Circus will be in the New England area only through August, and I wanted to offer you this opportunity to book them for your summer picnic at a specially discounted block booking rate."

Again, if you have a computer, you can use a form letter application for this, and personalize it with each recipient's name and address and salutation, as well as special clauses and paragraphs. In my seasonal letters, I include a line about it being "time to book entertainment for your

_____," and have the computer fill in the blanks with information from the client's record.

» *If It's Worth the Stamp ...*

Whether it's a mass mailing or individualized mailing, one rule of thumb I use in putting it together is that, since I'm spending 50¢ or more to mail each one, I'm sure as hell going to put 50¢ worth of literature inside. A client won't notice or appreciate the stamp, so why spend more on it than what's inside? Of course, with emails today, the cost of stamps isn't even a consideration.

» *6 Ways to Make Sure Your Mail Gets Opened and Read*

You've probably heard that one of the biggest challenges facing companies using direct mail is to get people to open the envelope. Junk and bulk-rate mail look just like the name implies, and are instant candidates for the "round file".

Your mailings can avoid this unseemly fate if you take special care with your envelopes:

- Address your mailings so that they look to be personally typed (labels project the opposite image, but I realize there are times when you can't avoid them).
- Don't use Bulk Mail or preprinted Business Permit mailing. But do use commemorative stamps–the larger and more colorful, the better. And if the Postal Service releases an appropriate stamp, such as the Performing Arts, Broadway Musicals, or Country Western Performers series of recent years–stock up on them.
- Use colored or specially imprinted envelopes.
- Paste on stickers and/or hand stamp "FIRST CLASS" or "IMPORTANT" on the front.
- Use such tricks as making it look like a telegram.
- Include a photo montage of some of your most eye-catching acts.

» *Weight Considerations*

Postage costs being what they are, if you're using snail mail you'll want to keep the weight of your mailing piece to a minimum. If you want to keep under the 1 oz. limit (one first-class stamp), include no more than four average-weight sheets, print everything on both sides, and design it as a self-mailer (no envelope needed).

If you anticipate doing a substantial amount of direct mail (500+ pieces each quarter), check with your post office about ways to reduce postage costs such as discounts for zip code sorting, and other available money-saving options.

» *Automating Your Mailings*

There are a number of ways to circumvent having to hand-address every envelope you send out:

- If you have access to a computer, use its list-processing ability to print your address labels or envelopes automatically.
- Use multi-part (with carbons) address label sheets, or type up one original set of address labels and then photocopy them onto address label sheets (special address

labels, designed to feed through a photocopier, can be purchased at most stationery stores and office supply houses).

- Use a labeling machine to imprint your envelopes.

» *The All-Important Follow-up*

No matter what type of mailing you do, remember that dropping your letters in the mailbox is not the end of the job, it's only the beginning. Direct mail alone rarely makes a sale; it is truly effective only if you follow up on it. So keep a list of your mailings, and be sure to follow up by phone in the next week or two.

Telemarketing: Reach Out and Sell Someone!

The phone is probably the most effective sales tool you possess. It's also the one you probably neglect the most. And it's probably the one you have the greatest fear of using. Mail offers a certain anonymity, but the phone puts you right on the "front lines", almost face-to-face with your prospect, and that can be downright scary.

With the Do Not Call laws that are in place, it's a bit risky making unsolicited calls, but most people will not object if you are courteous, pleasant, and targeted. For example, calling a business to ask about an upcoming promotional event and asking for the person in charge would probably be OK.

» *5 Tips for Telemarketing Success*

You can read lots of books on telephone technique, but keep these few tips in mind for starters:

1. Remind yourself that you're doing the prospect a favor. In many cases the person you're calling is someone who has multiple "slots" to fill, perhaps a month of activities, or even an entire season or year. Maybe it's someone who was drafted into chairing an entertainment committee, and this is a first-time experience for them. And maybe they're looking for the easiest, quickest way out. You can help them! When you begin to see things this way, you'll feel renewed confidence in yourself and the service you're providing.
2. Have some idea of what you're going to say before you start dialing. Who you are, whom you plan to ask for, why you happen to be calling at this time, which performers you're going to pitch, and what their fees and availabilities are.
3. Psyche yourself up! Get excited about what you're selling! You want to come across as professional, well-organized (an I've-got-the-best-damned-acts-in-the-business attitude), self-assured, and ready to solve their problem. And have your booking calendar, performer and client information sheets handy.
4. Make every call count! If you're not having any luck getting work from the person at the other end of the line, ask about what else is happening. Even if you don't get business from them this time, don't forget to ask what's coming up in the next few months, when you should check back with them, if there's anyone else you might call, and note all this in your records. Also remember that many of the people you'll be calling are involved in a number of other organizations and activities during the year, so fish around for opportunities.

5. Keep a record of your calls. Using your Contact File Client Information Form or a similar form, make a note of each call: whom you talked with, a summary of the conversation, what items were agreed to, and what steps should be taken as a result.

Nailing Down a Contract

Assuming that you get a "hot one" and a prospect actually buys, here's what you have to do while you still have them on the phone:

1. Get all the details about the job and the client down on paper. Ask the classic questions, "Who, What, Why, When"—they apply as much to a gig as they do to a well-written news item.
2. Among other things, be sure you find out the date, time, environment, whom the performer should ask for and where to find that person, equipment provided (stage, sound, lights, etc.), and everything else the performer needs to know (see "Getting It for the Record", Chapter 5).
3. Also find out the person and/or organization responsible for contracting and paying for the act, and the mailing address to which the contract and other correspondence is to be sent. It'll save you a lot of telephoning later, and reduce the possibility of missing or wrong information.
4. Give the buyer all the details he or she needs. Include a brief description of the act and its length, the act's proper stage name (spell it out if there's any doubt) and legal name, the kind of space and equipment required, what publicity materials you can supply, the exact fee being charged, and the deposit (if any) required and when it's due.

You'll be including most of this information on the contract you'll be sending out (see "Contracts and Other Necessary Evils", Chapter 5), but it's important that you and the buyer hammer out the basic agreement before you hang up the phone.

Advertising

With few exceptions, conventional advertising is probably the most expensive way of doing business. But there are times when you *should* consider it, especially if your goal is to achieve growth over a short period.

No matter what type of advertising you decide to use, we strongly recommend that you do the following:

- Monitor the response to each ad. Don't hesitate to pull an ad that's not producing. I know—it's tempting to just let an ad run on and on, but if you haven't received a hit after 5 or 6 runs, you're probably wasting your money.
- Limit your ad expenditures (including printing of sales literature) to about 10-15% of your gross commissions. If you follow this rule of thumb, you'll find that you're plowing back a reasonable amount of your budget into promotion, yet at the same time avoiding the temptation to overspend (a mistake I made in my early days, because like everyone, I wanted to see my name in headlines).

» *The Web*

For much of my career as an agent, the Internet was either non-existent or in its infancy, so I never spent a lot of time worrying about it. But today, its usefulness probably exceeds that of all other forms of advertising. It's become a *necessity*, and you should spend a serious amount of time and effort in creating an image that reflects well on you and your agency.

— *What do I need and what will it cost?*

I'm not going to spend a lot of time talking about the details of how to go about constructing your site, because there are plenty of tools and help out there. Basically you'll probably need to buy a "package" that provides you with a *domain*, a *hosting site*, and some *design tools*. One of the best website providers is Go Daddy (www.godaddy.com), which takes you through an automated process to determine what you need. The basics would ring up (in 2009 figures) as:

.COM Domain Name (e.g., *my-agency-name*.com) registration, 2 yrs $20.00
Private Registration Services, 2 yrs $15.00
Economy Hosting – Linux, 1 yr. $50.00

bringing you to around $90. This includes a 5-page website, and one personalized email address– you can expand these for an additional charge.

One important aspect of having a successful website is how easily people can find you. For example, if someone Googles "entertainment agency", will your name appear at the top of the listing or 50 pages down the line? Getting your name at the top depends on SEO (Search Engine Optimization), and you can purchase a Traffic Blazer option ($29.99/year) from Go Daddy to ensure that it does.

— *Website content*

What your site looks like and what it contains is pretty flexible, but check out competitors' sites for some ideas. You'll find that most sites offer the following at minimum:

- **About Us**–Who you are and what you do, and why you're the best choice to service their needs.
- **Talent Roster**–Some agencies list every act they represent, in detail, while others simply mention categories, such as Music, Vaudeville, Speakers Bureau, Circuses, Models. And don't forget to mention how new talent interested in hooking up with your agency can contact you.
- **Services**–Do you cater to weddings, offer birthday party packages, stage theme parties, or supply videography or photography services?
- **Testimonials** from Satisfied Clients–Very important. You don't have to list hundreds, but a half-dozen of the best can be enough to make them want to call *you*.
- **Contact Us**–OK, someone's interested in your lineup, so how to they contact you? This can be as simple as listing your address, phone #, and email address, or you can make this more elaborate by providing a form to fill out online.

» *Print Media*

Earlier in this chapter I suggested ways of developing leads, and some of them involved having listings or ads in various trade publications. If you decide to try this route, you're going to have to experiment a bit to find out which publications pay off for you. Some print media are measurably more effective than others.

In my own experience, I've found the following to be true:

— *Arts directories*

Advertising more than pays for itself here, because many of these directories are distributed to schools, recreation departments, libraries, museums, and other places which use them as their "yellow pages" when they're looking for entertainment. Space is relatively cheap, sometimes as low as $50-60 for a full-page ad, and most such publications have a "life" of a year or more.

— *Entertainment trade magazines, newsletters, show business directories, and special supplements*

Not a particularly good buy, because these publications are read (for the most part) by entertainers and their agents, not by buyers. However, some large alternative weeklies occasionally run a special Bands supplement, which will list you and your acts for free. But be prepared to get a raft of calls from every band in your area wanting to know "if you'd like to handle us".

Also, many of the show-biz directories such as *Cavalcade of Acts & Attractions*, will list you and your acts for free, but again, be prepared for an avalanche of calls from bands "looking for an agent"–which is fine if you're short on bands, but a nuisance if you're not.

— *Advertising and marketing journals*

A good way to reach advertising agencies, and marketing and promotional managers if you have some acts that can be used in promotions (grand openings, trade shows, shopping malls and other retail outlets, etc.). You can run either a display ad or a listing in their Suppliers directory section.

— *Newspaper classifieds*

I know a lot of entertainers who consistently run "business card ads" (usually nothing more than a 1-line description of their act, plus their name and phone number) in the classified section of their local daily or weekly rag. Most admit they just want to get their name in print and that such ads are not a success from a profit standpoint. A classified's chief virtue is that it's cheap (usually only $10-25 a run), and can be considered a kind of corporate advertising (advertising whose main purpose is to keep a company's name and image in the public's mind). I'd suggest limiting such ads to the peak buying season, September-December.

— *Phone book "yellow pages"*

A powerful but expensive medium, but it's sort of obligatory if people are to take you seriously. If you decide to do this, be particular about which regional editions you choose. Better to start with one or two, and expand from there. Beware the pseudo-Yellow Pages, those directories published by other than the official Yellow Pages publisher. People are still inclined to use the real thing, and throw away the impostors.

NOTE: The ad isn't your only cost—to qualify for a yellow pages listing, you must have a *business* phone installed, which costs almost double the rates of a residential phone.

A general caveat is to beware of any out-of-state calls received from your ads in national publications—the prospects usually sound sincere, and you spent lots of time and expense responding to their inquiries, but the people are usually just 'window-shopping' and price-comparing, and such deals rarely reach fruition.

For example, do you seriously think a California agency really has to import a less-than-top-draw magician all the way from Massachusetts when there are thousands of magicians already out there on the West Coast? Yet I get calls like that all the time. Maybe they've been doing a lot of late nights and they're not thinking clearly when they call, but when they finally come to their senses, they quickly forget about me and turn to local sources.

— Airing on the airwaves

At one time, radio and TV would have been well beyond your budget, but today with less costly FM radio, local cable, and webcasts and podcasts proliferating across the nation, you might want to consider them. I've never used them myself, so I can't speak from first-hand experience, but I suspect they reach too broad an audience to be very cost effective. Also, I don't know of any other agencies that use these vehicles.

On the top local AM radio stations, rates can run into the hundreds of dollars for a 30-second ad during morning or evening drive time. TV rates I don't even want to talk about. And don't forget the cost of producing the ad in the first place.

Some of the best buys in radio are on the FM stations, especially those that are college-affiliated. Check with those in your area as to rates and availabilities. Many, however, are non-profit and may not accept advertising.

One avenue you might consider here is cable television, particularly your town's public access channel, where residents can produce and air their own programs. Also, most cable systems have a bulletin-board channel that displays a series of "recipe-card" ads over and over again.

Other than that, anything else is probably out of the question, budget-wise. But as more and more specially targeted channels come on board the cable systems, who knows? Maybe rates will drop to an affordable level. Unfortunately, you must be willing to repeat your ad until the viewing audience reaches an awareness level, so be prepared to hang in there for the long haul.

If you need help in producing your radio or TV ads, you might want to talk to the Communications departments at your local colleges. You'll find that there are scores of talented, creative students eager to do ads, sometimes for the experience or class credits or their portfolios, other times for a very low fee.

Internships (unpaid positions designed to give students practical experience in their chosen career) are a great way to get the assistance you need, both in this and other areas (see "Watch Out, Jay Leno, Here I Come!" in Chapter 5 for another example of using interns).

— *Bulletin boards, directories, and other "free" media*

Well, actually not entirely free, as you'll have to invest some money in printing and, unless you do it yourself, in distribution. Bulletin boards—in colleges, supermarkets, copy centers, activity rooms in apartment and condo complexes—offer another way to advertise your services, and all for the investment of a little shoe leather.

You should print your ads on 3x5 index cards (brightly "neon" colored, if possible), or you may decide to just tack up your business card. If it appears you need permission to post your ad, get it–otherwise your ad may mysteriously and quickly disappear.

Leaflet distribution may offer you another way to get your name before the public. Pass them out door-to-door, hand them out at places where potential customers tend to gather, and drop them off at local business establishments, churches, clubs, and other places.

» *Trade Shows, Festivals, & Conventions*

I've already mentioned the National Association of College Activities, the various State and County Fair Associations, and other places that sponsor talent showcases that you can take advantage of. There are also conventions run by the Country Music Association, the International Association of Auditorium Managers, the International Association of Amusement Parks and Attractions, the International Association of Fairs and Expositions, and many others at the regional and state levels..

Besides the showcases, most of these gatherings provide an exhibit area where you can set up a booth. To get the most bang for your buck, you should do both: showcase one or more acts, *and* have a booth where prospects can go after the show for more information.

— *Costs*

Be forewarned: this can cost big time! Many of these associations require that you become a member and pay your annual dues in addition to plunking down the cost of the showcase fee and booth space. As an example, let's total up a typical "convention package":

- Annual membership dues ($200 and up)
- Booth Space ($250 and up)
- Convention Registration, i.e., the admission fee ($75 and up)
- Booth Furniture, which includes table, chairs, etc. (rental or purchase, $100 and up)
- Union fees for moving your materials into and out of the exhibit hall.
- Union fees for hooking you up to electricity, telephone, and other services.
- Poster, signage, and other booth decorations.
- Printed sales literature, advertising specialties, and other give-aways
- Showcase fees ($200 and up)
- Transportation, lodging, food, and other on-the-road expenses for you and your performer(s) if the showcase site is remote.

Add it all up, and you can see that you can easily spend $2,500 on just one event. Odds are you won't recoup your investment the first time around, but you may get enough exposure and contacts to make up for it in other ways.

— Competition

At many conventions, you'll be up against the Big Guys, and I guarantee you'll feel pretty insignificant when you see their multi-thousand-dollar booths, their army of 3-piece-suited sales people, the top line acts they're promoting, and the extravagant freebies they hand out.

At one convention, I was next to none other than the William Morris Agency (about as big as they come), and they handed out record albums and full-color posters for three days without stopping. (At least they drew the crowds and I was able to trap some of them for a moment as they passed by.) On the positive side, consider that trade shows and conventions offer a great way to:

- Get a behind-the-scenes look at the entertainment industry and rub elbows with its denizens. Despite their cut-throat reputation, most show-biz people are actually quite nice and are willing to help if you approach them in the right way.
- Learn some of the tricks of the trade by watching those agencies bigger and more experienced than you.
- See what other acts are out there and maybe add a few new ones to your own roster. Be sure to attend the showcases whenever possible, visit the other booths, and take any promo material that looks interesting.
- Meet some of the big names in entertainment. Through conventions I've had a chance to talk with such internationally acclaimed magicians as The Amazing Randi and. Harry Blackstone, Jr. (both of whom gave me private demonstrations of some of their latest illusions), and to briefly introduce myself to Red Skelton, Simon and Garfunkle, the Smothers Brothers, and Leonard Nimoy.

But there are less expensive arenas in which you can showcase your talent, set up a booth, and strut your stuff: local Chamber of Commerce "fairs", shopping malls, advertising and industrial shows, parks and recreation department conventions, and other commercial and trade get-togethers. The fees are much more reasonable, there are usually no membership requirements, and the sites are usually close enough to home that travel and lodging expenses will be nil.

— Spots to avoid

When you're booking your space at an exhibit or convention, and you're selecting your space, avoid locations that are:

- Plagued with obstructing columns
- Dead-end aisles
- Under balconies, overhangs, or other types of low ceilings
- Near loading docks or freight doors
- In poorly lit areas
- In "late setup" areas.

You may pay a premium for premium space, but remember the old real estate slogan regarding the three most important features of property: "Location, location, location"!

— *8 items to always bring with you*

Regardless of the convention or event, there are some basic things you'll need as a conventioneer:

- A layout plan to use every square inch of exhibit space effectively. Most exhibit spaces are 8'x10'.
- A folding table (3x6' or 3x8' should be sufficient). You can find these at most discount office suppliers for around $40-60. A good investment anyway, because you can find dozens of uses for it around the house when it's not on the road.
- Display panels (table top, or floor-height) on which you can mount posters, glossies, signs, and brochures. You can make these yourself out of heavy Bristol-board (mount large panels on 1x2" studs); and paint them in vivid colors.
- Large banners and other signage (Bristol board, cloth, or heavy-duty paper), with the name of your agency, town, state, and phone number.
- Sales literature. Be well-stocked (what you don't use you can take back home) with printed materials. Have at hand a general brochure or sheet on the agency, plus individual pieces on the performers you're showcasing or otherwise featuring.
- Advertising specialties such as calendars, pens, coins, etc., all imprinted with your agency name, address, and phone number of course.
- Audio-Visual Equipment. Either a combination TV/DVR to play videos of your acts, or an automatic, carousel-type, rear-screen slide/sound projector. You'll have to film a video or set up a slide show of your best acts, and then add some narrative and background music. Make it colorful, loud, and attention-getting. To purchase either of these devices would cost you in the range of $400-600, so you'll probably want to rent them instead. Sometimes you'll be required to use headphones for the audio, so it won't disturb your fellow exhibitors, but I don't think that's a problem.
- Visitor Cards or Guest Book. For recording information on the visitors to your booth. Provide space for their name, affiliation, address, phone number, and their particular interests. Later, after you get home, you can follow up any promising leads by phone or letter, and also add this information to your records for future mailings.

— *Five tips on getting results from your booth*

Here are some general tips for getting the most out of your participation in a trade show:

- Promote your appearance at the show. You can do pre-show promotional mailings, give prospective attendees a call, run ads in publications likely to be read by the attendees. The sponsor of the show can usually provide you with a list of members or invitees that you can employ in your campaign. Some offer a "program guide" to the exhibits and speakers, in which you can purchase ad space.
- Bring along additional literature to hand out just prior to each showcase performance (assuming that you're showcasing one or more acts). Showcases are frequently scheduled during or after the convention banquet, or in some other sit-down environment, so I usually distribute literature packets on each table (or chair). If the setting is a large

auditorium, you can either place this literature on the seats or stand by the door and hand them out as people come into the hall.

- Be at your booth and be alert during exhibit hours. Make every minute count—it's your turn to be in the spotlight, so think of yourself as a performer and wow your audience.
- Aggressively button-hole people into your booth as they pass by. Just as you avoid the pitchmen at a carnival, or the appliance sales people at Sears, many of the attendees will be gun-shy and try to avoid you, but use your charm and they'll warm up. After all, if you don't make contact, you might as well stay home. A convention or exhibit frequently resembles a carnival midway, with each "barker" trying to beat out the competition.
- Keep up on what's happening. Check the bulletin boards posted in the conference areas, attend all exhibitor meetings, and keep your ears open. Because of their size, conventions are not the most organized events you'll ever come across, and exhibit hours, rules, showcase times, locations, and other things have a way of changing from day to day. And sometimes there are penalties if you don't adhere to the agenda, such as failing to attend a meeting or not being at your booth during exhibit hours.

» *Creating Your Own Promo Events*

If you can't find such opportunities, create them! Any place that people gather or hold regular meetings is a possibility. Ask one of the shopping malls near you if you can rent space for a display or booth. Talk to church, civic, municipal, and industrial groups about setting up at one of their meetings.

As a personal example, one time I contacted a Parks and Recreation association that represented all of the parks and recreation directors in all of the cities and towns in Eastern Mass, and asked them if they'd let me organize a talent showcase for their next annual convention. They were happy to assent, and I was able to put on a full showcase of my acts, which resulted in plenty of summer bookings. (Unfortunately, that being my first time, I scheduled way too many acts and didn't allow for setup and knockdown time, and when we reached the last act, only about 10 people still remained in the audience.)

Sales Calls

If you're doing this on a part-time basis and have a regular 9-to-5 job, you'll find that making sales calls is an almost impossible task.

But if you're a full-timer or work your other job in the off hours, making in-person sales calls is a powerful way to garner business. There's almost nothing else that's as effective as a face-to-face presentation. A personal visit:

- Makes you and your agency more "real" and memorable than letters and phone calls, and establishes a relationship between you and the prospect.
- Enables you to get better acquainted with a prospect's situation, site, and needs.
- Permits a more extensive repertoire in your presentation, including video, slides, films,

If such areas lie within your target market, I'd give top priority to visiting the student activity offices at colleges and universities, the principals of grade schools, and directors of recreation departments. These are the prospects can provide multiple contracts during the year and represent your best return on investment.

There are many books on how to sell successfully, and you can peruse them if you want to, but the most important tip I can give you is to be friendly, polite, and low-key (but enthusiastic), and show a sincere desire to be of assistance. Booking agents have a reputation of being "hard-sell", and everyone gets their defenses up when they see a sales person approaching, so surprise them by being just the opposite of what they're expecting!

Promotion

Entertainment is a business of *promotion*, so you shouldn't neglect promoting your agency and yourself. With all the noise and clamor around us, sometimes it takes the ingenuity of a P. T. Barnum to get attention these days.

Don't be afraid to use your imagination—it may be one of the most important keys to success. Below are some of the methods I've considered (and in some cases, used) over the years.

» *Guest Spots on Radio and TV Talk Shows*

Get your performers on TV and radio, particularly the local segments of those "magazine shows" such as *The Today Show, Good Morning America, Evening Magazine*, and the like. Or try getting them on radio programs directed toward an act's specialty—like a folk music or jazz program.

In my own experience, I established a good rapport with several magazine shows. *Evening Magazine* devoted entire segments (including their Boston debut) to my street performers. A Public Broadcasting System series features my acts on a regular basis. A Boston network TV station also frequently invites my acts as guests. On radio, a number of college stations have had my musicians on their folk music programs, which sometimes devote as much as an hour to a single guest. And I'm also an unofficial "scout" for the producers of *Geraldo*, a program on which I've appeared myself.

— *Come Up with an "Angle"*

If this is something you feel might be beneficial, the way to start the ball rolling is to think up a convincing "angle", then call up and talk with the producer (or assistant producer) of an appropriate show. And by "appropriate", I mean a program that frequently features the genre or idea you're offering. If they evince some interest, send them a press kit and then follow up a few days later with another phone call.

Once you've hit pay dirt and gotten an act on the program, roll out the publicity and tell all your clients to watch (or listen to) the program—they'll be able to "audition" your act without leaving their living rooms.

— *Benefits of Radio and TV*

Besides exposure, there are several side benefits to getting on radio or TV: Usually the station will provide you with a copy of the audio or video and you can use it in future sales endeavors. And it's another item to add to the act's (and your) résumé.

Of course, *you* can be featured on these shows as well as your acts. Being a talent agent is certainly an unconventional occupation, making you a potential interviewee. If you have some good tales to tell of your experiences, all the better. Just mail a 1-piece release to the shows, telling why you'd make an interesting guest.

» *Socializing with the Socialites*

Approach some of the Perle Mesta's of your area and ask them to remember you when they're putting together one of their private soirees or other extravaganza. They'll probably be most interested in nice quiet combos to play unobtrusively in the corner of the Grand Salon (or whatever they call their living room).

As you can imagine, socialites can be very interesting people to get to know, and they're not as intimidating as they may appear. If you can be of service to them, they'll be happy to talk with you.

For example, I've dealt with a leading party-giver for many years, someone who's very active in putting on private parties, charity affairs, and just about everything else on the Boston social scene. One time I met with her to discuss her upcoming parties and, as we talked, she turned the conversation to her daughter, who had been thinking of taking the family's antique hurdy-gurdy and doing an "organ grinder sans monkey" act on the streets for the summer, and asked if I had any suggestions. I gave her some advice (including the idea of her daughter dressing up as the monkey, thinking that a "monkey" cranking his own hurdy-gurdy would be a clever twist).

» *Hosting Your Own Talent Showcase*

Earlier, I mentioned the idea of putting on a mini-showcase at a meeting of some club or other organization. I also mentioned that various associations, such as Fair associations, sponsor their own showcases of talent. Combine these two ideas, and consider putting on your own Performer Showcase and target it at a particular industry or group. All you have to do is:

- Select a suitable site (a small auditorium, for example)
- Choose the acts to showcase
- Obtain whatever lighting and sound will be required
- Provide some sort of refreshment or lunch (optional)
- Assemble a sales literature packet for the attendees to take home.
- Send out the invitations

Putting on your own showcase can be fun, and quite effective if you handle it right. It will also give you some valuable insights into what it's like to be on the other side of the fence, as a club manager, producer, or theater owner. It also lets you take full control, rather than working within the rules of (and paying fees to) some outside sponsoring organization.

» *Getting Free Newspaper Coverage*

Remember that newspapers are for more than running ads—they print features, articles, and columns, and you and your acts can be highlighted in some of them if you make the effort.

As an example, I began Chapter 1 with quotes from various feature articles written about my agency, from newspapers right there in Massachusetts to a rag way out in Seattle.

55

» *Helping Your Client to Publicize an Event*

Most of the time your client is responsible for publicizing an event, but there are things you can do to help. For example, if it's a public event, find out what publicity they're planning and ask what you can contribute in the way of bio's, photos, and such. If the event is written up afterwards, try to get a copy for your own files and for possible use as part of a mailing or a press kit. If the organization sponsoring the event is printing up programs, posters, or leaflets, push to get a listing, photo, or write-up of your act included.

» *Publicizing Your Own Acts*

If one of your performers has an interesting story to tell, try to interest a newspaper in printing it. Editors are always interested in human interest stories, and if you can find an angle, they'll find the space. Some of the articles in which my performers have been highlighted include:

- **Street Performers "Band" Together**—The rewards and perils, and how local street entertainers are forming their own cooperative union to fight harassment.
- **Down the Hatch Without a Scratch**—Sword-swallowing, viewed from a medical perspective, and illustrated by actual X-rays taken at a major Boston hospital.
- **Brother Blue, Who Are You?**—A professor at Harvard Divinity School, with a doctorate from Yale, who dresses up in balloons, bells, and gaily colored streamers to become the zany Brother Blue.
- **Witches, Ghosts, and the Paranormal**—Many of my Wiccan, ghost hunting, and psychic speakers are featured in Halloween-related articles every year.

There are also many opportunities to get your agency some free publicity. Perhaps your local papers occasionally do articles on small businesses in the area. If so, convince an editor that your business is one of the most fascinating and newsworthy around. If you're supplying acts to a charity or fund-raiser, see if you can get a credit in the program or a mention in the newspaper coverage. Also, stores using your acts as promotions would probably consider including a photo of your act in their ad or article.

» *Using Charitable Events for Promotion*

I just mentioned charities and fund raisers, and I'd like to say a bit more about them.

I'd strongly recommend that you selectively book some of your acts into well-attended, high-brow charity functions and other worthy causes. The pay may be next to nothing (and sometimes even nothing), but what you're actually doing (don't tell anybody) is showcasing your act before a very influential and well-heeled audience–and you know who throws those really big bashes, don't you? As examples, I've booked acts at the Footlight Theater Parade and Costume Ball, a fund-raiser for Boston's Theater District that's attended by the elite of the Hub.

Also try to get on some of those TV fund-raisers, like those perennial auctions run by your local PBS station. If the idea is to donate a prize to be auctioned off, consider donating one of your lower-priced acts, such as the services of a clown or magician for a birthday party. Or, if it's a show like the *Jerry Lewis Telethon for Muscular Dystrophy*, offer to have some of your acts come on the show to entertain.

Chapter 4
Selling and Negotiating

You've combed your area for prospects, you've done your mailings and made your phone calls, and now you're starting to get some action. How do you handle it? What are the secrets to successfully closing the sale? And how do you go about setting a price that will please both the buyer and the performer? In this chapter, we'll be talking about:

- Projecting the image of an "entertainment expert"
- Weaving a tale to "sell the sizzle"
- Impressing the client
- Negotiating the fee within the boundaries of the act's needs and the client's budget

You're the Expert

Just to boost your self-confidence a bit, let me remind you that *the majority of people you'll be dealing with have never booked entertainment before.* Instead, they've volunteered for (or been drafted into) student activities programming, the Town Day Committee, the Annual Mother-and-Daughter Banquet, or the local Arts & Crafts Fair. Or they're hosting a birthday party, planning a wedding or an anniversary celebration, or the Grand Opening of their gift shop.

In any case, they know next to nothing about hiring entertainment, and that's why they've come to you.

Like it or not, you've been cast in the role of Entertainment Expert, so talk and act like one. Be prepared and willing to give recommendations. As one of my form letters states, "We've been in the business for over 30 years, and we know what works .... and what doesn't." And after a few years, you'll know, too. Always draw on your past experience—it's one of your most valuable assets.

When someone calls you, they want to be reassured that whatever they buy from you is guaranteed to be successful. So, when possible, recommend acts that have proven themselves in similar circumstances and tell them that's what you're doing. I have a few acts I routinely pitch to certain clients, and they're almost always successful.

Let's say an ocean-front tourist attraction is having an Opening Day celebration. I suggest my Gypsy Fiddler & Dancing Bear act. Why? Because it's a good, crowd-pleasing act, and because it is associated with the sea. (Back in the days of Far East Trade, sea captains would bring back trained bears as souvenirs of faraway ports of call, and then either hired them out or sold them to gypsies who would then exhibit them on the streets of the seacoast towns.) Or I might pitch a folk music group that includes a healthy portion of sea chanteys in their repertoire.

A Story is Worth a Thousand Words

One powerful sales trick is weaving a spellbinding story about an act into your sales pitch. Get the prospect to imagine what a thrill it would be to present an act at their upcoming event. In sales parlance, that's called "Selling the Sizzle instead of the Steak". Or, as I like to phrase it, "Create a dream, then sell it".

For example, if I'm trying to sell Capt. Don, my tattooed sword-swallower and fire-eater, I may talk a bit about some of the close calls he's experienced over the years, or explain how he mixes a concoction of diesel fuel, gasoline, and gun powder for his Human Volcano finale—a "rolling, rumbling fireball of flame that shoots 40 feet or more from his mouth!" I may add that "he's tattooed everywhere, even on the inside of his lips!".

If I'm pitching The Gloucester Hornpipe and Clog Society, I never fail to mention that rarely seen (and even more rarely heard) instrument, the Pogo-Cello, "a folk instrument invented by a crazed druggist from New Jersey, and built from a carved staff, a cow bell, piano wire, lids from some cat food cans, and a cookie tin". In addition, even their name provides a topic of conversation: "No, they don't come from Gloucester, and a 'clog' is a dance, not a shoe. Early in their career, before they had a name, they were about to play one night, and the m.c. asked how he should introduce them. As they happened to be in Gloucester, and their first piece was a hornpipe and clog number, one of the members responded, "Oh, just say that we're the Gloucester Hornpipe and Clog Society", and the name stuck.

Speaking of evocative names, how about these: Sumitra, Scrub-Board Slim, We Tickle the Earth's Belly, The Ha-Ha Puppet Theater, Do'A, Pif, and RuthAnna the Sweet Singer of Beacon Hill. Yes, there are stories behind every one of those names, and I exploit them to the hilt. Then there's Mr. Fingers, who took his name from the fact that as a child he had to use sign language to communicate with his parents, both of whom were deaf mutes. And there's also The Narrow Land String Band, so named because they call Cape Cod their home.

How about Bob the Organ Grinder? Did you know that his hurdy gurdy is over 100 years old and worth thousands of dollars? And that Jo-Jo, his monkey, is a 16-year-old Capuchin who took years to train, and can't perform outdoors if the temperature is below 50 degrees because he's sensitive to the cold? And that, since Federal law prohibits the transport of monkeys across state lines, monkeys (and any offspring) are usually handed down in families from father to son?

Sgt. Pepperoni's One-Man Band also provides a wealth of fascinating "hooks". He comes "bedecked with over 30 instruments—bass drums, accordion, cow bells, flutes, harmonica, cymbals, and horns—plus blocks, which he plays with a drumstick attached to the back of his head. He holds the World's Record of playing 12 instruments simultaneously!" Unforgettable? You bet!

Stephen Baird, the #1 Street Singer of Boston? I tell about the time he was sitting on a park bench on the campus of the college where he was pursuing a degree in nuclear physics. He was playing around with his guitar, and singing along to himself, when a well-dressed man approached and sat down at the other end of the bench. He stayed a while, listening to the music, and when he stood up, he dropped something into Stephen's hat, which was laying on the bench beside him. Later, when Stephen was gathering up his things to return to the dorm, he discovered that the man had dropped a $50 bill into the chapeau, and right then and there decided to change his career goal from nuclear physicist to street entertainer!

Brother Blue, whom I mentioned back in Chapter 3, is an ordained Episcopalian minister and an associate pastor at a church in Boston's Back Bay. Festooned in multi-colored balloons, tassels, silver rings, and streamers, and with a knit beret set rakishly on his head and a butterfly tattoo on his cheek, he plays the role of a modern-day prophet and preaches in parables on the streets of Boston, in a way that is both entertaining and spell-binding. He holds a Doctor of Divinity degree from Yale, and is on the staff of the Harvard Divinity School in Cambridge. Let me tell you, it makes people's mouths water just wanting to book him.

Can you dress up stories a bit, exaggerate perhaps? Sure, but be basically honest. For example, you can say that an act "performed at the White House by special invitation" or "put on a command performance at Buckingham Palace" even though they were one of a dozen or more such acts.

Impressing the Client: Whom Do You Know & Where Have You Been?

Has the act performed as an opener for some celebrity, or appeared at some well-known place, or been associated with someone famous? Mention it!

For example, if I'm talking about Jon Stetson, one of my magicians, I may casually mention that he performed by invitation for Jimmy Carter at the White House. (And the prospect thinks, "Gee, if he's good enough for the President ...")

Or I'll inform them that Capt. Don once toured with the Munchkins of "Wizard of Oz" fame, or that a staff member of the Ha-Ha Puppet Theater once auditioned for Jim Henson, creator of the Muppets. Even if Jim had auditioned 200 others that day (which he didn't), it still sounds impressive, right?

Of course I'll always point out that Barbara Autry is the sister of that famed "Singing Cowboy", Gene Autry, and that she appeared with him in his TV series as well as at his rodeos. (In reality, she's his *half*-sister, but why split hairs?) And when she opens with the crooning sounds of "I'm Back in the Saddle Again" in the background, it's almost like old Gene is there in person.

I also once had an actress who was a direct descendent of Macbeth (yes, Macbeth was a real person, a king of Scotland in the 11th century—look him up in an encyclopedia if you don't believe me. And you might remember that another of his descendants, the present Earl of Cawdor was featured prominently in ads for s certain brand of Scotch whiskey). I don't know if this relationship added to her acting ability, but it sure was worth mentioning.

If you think that your acts can't match these legends, just ask them. You might be surprised at some of the tales they can tell you. And if they don't have a gimmick, start developing one.

Negotiating the Fee

As I explained back in the discussion on commissions in Chapter 2, you can either deduct your commission from the performer's standard fee or you can tack it on top. The decision is between you and the act.

» *Set Consistent Fees*

Ideally, the fee you quote should be the same fee the performer would quote if contacted directly by the prospect. That way, if the prospect asks whether he or she is paying the commission, you can explain to them that they're not. That, in fact, they're getting the benefit of your expertise and services absolutely free.

One of the ways you earn your commission is to act as a negotiator/mediator and reach a mutually acceptable agreement on the fee. Under the subject of "Fees" in Chapter 2,. I urged that the act work up a reasonable fee schedule and then stick to it. However, be sure to ask about the minimum fee an act will accept, and use it as your "ace in the hole" when you have no other alternative.

» *Fuzzy Math*

Sometimes, after you've quoted the standard rate for a 2-hour performance, or a day or whatever, your prospect will come back with "Well, we only want them for an hour ... how much for only an hour?" As I explained under "Fees" back in Chapter 2, an hour really isn't an hour, and isn't charged at half the price of two hours. **Any performance usually represents a day's work for most acts, and takes the same amount of preparation and energy, regardless of the actual length of the performance.** Don't forget that there's rehearsal time, travel time, set-up time, makeup and dressing time, etc., in addition to the show itself. And most performers don't want to travel all over the countryside to several different jobs in one day.

And therein lies the problem. Most of your clients do not book entertainment as their primary duty. So they have a punch-the-time-clock perspective because that's how it is with their job. They think in terms of hourly pay, and they're comparing the hourly fee that you're asking with what they make. You can see the problem—how do you explain that your act is asking $250 for working one hour, while they may be making only $15 an hour plus benefits?

Here's how:

- An act doesn't work "only an hour". A 1-hour show takes much longer than that when you count in travel time, preparation time, setup time, and so forth.
- An act has invested many years in training and practice. And when an act rehearses for an upcoming show, it's not "on the clock".
- An act also must invest money for props and other equipment, and pay for all their transportation and other business expenses.
- An act gets no benefits such as health and accident insurance, paid holidays, sick days, 401K plans, pensions, long-term disability, and vacations that most employees receive for free. And they have to pay a Self-Employment Tax that's nearly double what an employed person pays for FICA or Social Security.

So—you must *educate* your clients and convince them that $250 "per hour" isn't as insane as it sounds at first. Remember: *Talent isn't baloney—you don't buy it by the pound!*

But also try to be sympathetic to your client's plight. The person you're dealing with will have to justify the fee to his or her superiors. Also, non-profit, charitable, and small organizations really do have limited budgets (and sometimes an act is willing to discount the fee for such groups).

» *Working within a Client's Budget*

I'll repeat: the act has the final say in accepting or rejecting a job. If a prospect says, "I can't afford more than X dollars, take it or leave it", no matter how ridiculously low that offer may be, you are obligated to tell the prospect that you don't think the act can afford to perform at that price but you'll run it by them anyway. Then, when you speak with the act, if they can't go along with the offer, see if they'll make a counter offer. When you stop to think about it, it's a lot like selling real estate: a real estate agent is a negotiator and must, by law, present any offer they get from a prospective buyer to the seller, and vice versa.

» *4 Ways to Save Your Client Money*

There are several ways to save a client some money without taking it out of the performer's pocket:

- If travel expenses are a key factor in the fee, suggest to the client that they try to arrange for a "block booking". Block booking simply means booking an act into several places in the same geographic area on the same day (or successive days), resulting in each buyer sharing the costs of transportation, lodging, and other expenses. In addition, many performers are willing to consider cutting their prices for a chance to work for 3 or 4 days straight.
- In large cities where street entertainers abound, and where people are more familiar with the practice of "passing the hat", you might suggest to the buyer that the performer be allowed to put out the hat as a way of earning a portion of the fee. In that case, the buyer agrees to make up the difference between the money received and the agreed-upon fee. Of course, this solution works only for situations where the audience is mobile, such as a street festival, a fair, or other outdoor event.
- If you're dealing with a non-profit or charitable institution, suggest that they solicit a sponsor for the show, and then work out some way that either they or your act can advertise the benefactor. A clown or animal character might hand out fliers or tokens on behalf of the sponsor, a juggler might add the sponsor's name to his props, or you could simply acknowledge the sponsor in some other way (a sign on the stage, a mention in the printed program, etc.).

» *Half a Loaf Is Better Than None*

You'll find I've repeated this adage several times in this book, because it's a very good philosophy to keep in mind. If the bid is for an entire package of acts, be sure to make it clear to your client that you can supply the whole package or any of its parts. Some agents operate on an all-or-nothing basis, but when you're just starting out, you can't afford to. Whenever possible, push to get at least a piece of the action. Then, if you do an exemplary job, next time you may be awarded a bigger piece.

If there's one business where it's important to get your foot in the door and to prove yourself, it's this one! After that, the rest is easy.

Chapter 5
Closing the Sale

In this Chapter:

As a wit once remarked about using the rest room (to put it euphemistically), "The job isn't over till the paper work is done". And how true that is in the entertainment business. We'll be talking about:

- Getting down all the necessary information–completely and accurately.
- Completing the contract, regardless of who issues it.
- Invoicing the client to collect the fee.

OK … your prospect, trusting in your impeccable expertise, has agreed to deal. Get out a pad of paper and a sharp pencil, and start jotting down the details.

Accuracy counts! If you transpose even one digit, you might find yourself sending out a performer on the 12th of July when the engagement is actually on the 21st, or collecting only a $350 fee when it should be $530. Or you might recall that the performance is in Hudson MA., when it's actually in Hudson, NH, or that the time of the performance is 9 AM when it's really 9 PM. And you don't what *that* to happen, do you?

And don't assume that your *selling* job is over. Some last-minute misunderstanding or change can still come along to tax your negotiating skills, tact, and patience. The client really meant to say that she wanted an hour-and-a-half performance, not just an hour. Or your client just booked your prime Fire-Eater and later discovered that the fire marshal won't allow an open flame in the auditorium. And no one remembered to talk about rain dates and how other "acts of God" should be handled.

Getting It for the Record –Filling Out the Contract

Once you've received the go-ahead on a job, be ready to write down all the picky little details you'll need to fill out the contract and provide the necessary information to the performer. In general, your "job information sheet" and the contract you'll create from it should have space for the following. Some items are discussed in greater detail later in this chapter. A sample copy of a blank contract is provided in Appendix B.

» *Name of the act*

The 'stage name' of the act, plus the 'real name' (if a group, the name of the leader or manager to whom the check should be written, if the group does not have a business account in its own name).

» *Name, address, phone # of the purchaser*

The official name of the organization or group which is hiring the act, plus their address and phone number. A cardinal rule is: the more phone numbers you can get, the better, so get both the business phone number and at least one home phone number. And get their email address.

» *Official representative*

The name of the person legally empowered to sign the contract.

» *Agreed fee and how paid*

The performance fee (see below). Accepting a check is perfectly OK, and I've never offered a credit-card option.

» *Performance day and date*

The day(s) of the week and the full calendar date(s) of the contracted performance. Putting down both is a good way to "double check" the information. Pull out your calendar and make sure the days and dates agree. It's not uncommon to get one or the other wrong. Also, you may have to agree to a rain date, an alternative date in case of bad weather.

» *Performance site and directions*

A detailed description of where the performer is to show up, and to whom they should report. I usually attach a note to the contract, asking the purchaser to send back a map with the signed copy, but try to obtain enough information so that a map is not absolutely necessary. Also, ask about parking, and if passes are needed to gain entrance.

» *Start time and length of the performance*

The start time and length of performance. See below for things to be considered.

» *Arrival time/setup/ rehearsal time*

Arrival time depends on (a) how much time is needed for setup of equipment, do sound and light checks, put on makeup and costume, and rehearse, (b) when the stage or other site will be open and available, and (c) when the purchaser would like to have the performer on hand for their convenience or peace of mind.

Even if a performer can go on "cold", the purchaser might like to have him or her show up 15 minutes early so there's time to go over any last minute details.

» *Special arrangements (Riders)*

Special agreements in addition to common contractual terms. See below for a list of some of these.

» *Agreed fee and how paid*

This section of the contract states the total performance fee charged to the client, and when, in what form, and to whom it is to be paid. For example, if the engagement is for three days at $500 per day and payment is to be made directly to the performer following the appearance, you'd write something like:

Three days @$500 = $1500.00 cash or check payable to the Brinkley Puppets and delivered on the last day of the engagement.

Sometimes, due to bookkeeping procedures and bureaucratic "red tape", you can't always get them to pay on the day of the performance, so you might have to rewrite the above to say:

Three days @$500 = $1500.00 cash or check payable to the Brinkley Puppets and due and payable no later than 14 days following the engagement.

Be aware that it may take as long as two to four weeks before you'll get a check. One municipality I dealt with took six months to pay! But don't worry unduly. Most organizations are trustworthy and pay their debts. If your performers start to fret, just remind them that it's "like money in the bank".

» *Who should be the payee?*

One decision you'll have to make is to whom should the check be payable–you or the performer? Personally, I prefer that all checks go directly to the performer, for several reasons:

The check can be handed over to them at the performance, rather than risk having it get lost in the mail.

It involves fewer trips to the bank and less bookkeeping for me. Also, it avoids my having to issue 1099s at the end of the year and doing more calculations on my tax returns.

Of course it means that you'll have to rely on the performer to send you your commission, but I've never had any trouble on that score.

If the check is to be made out to the performer, be sure that the purchaser has the performer's legal name (the name on the bank account). Technically, banks honor only checks made out to the exact name of the account, and many performers haven't taken the trouble to set up a separate "business account" under their stage name.

However, you'll find that some organizations feel safer giving you the check—after all, you're the person they've been dealing with—so go along with them. When income tax time comes around, you'll have to report the entire amount as income, and then offset it by listing the performer's net fee as "Other Expenses" on Schedule C. Note that you do not list them as "Wages", as the performers are not your employees.

» *Deposits*

What about asking for an advance deposit? In some cases, it might be very wise to insist on a deposit (down payment) for an engagement. For instance, it's a good idea to ask *new* clients for a deposit. And certain acts will require that you get a deposit before they consider the date to be booked.

If you plan to ask for a deposit, inform the purchaser of this fact while talking with them on the phone, and then enclose a note with the contract that the agreed deposit must be mailed back with the signed contract before the date is considered booked. Then, if an event is canceled or the terms of the contract are otherwise violated, you deduct an amount equal to (commission rate x deposit amount) to cover your expenses, and send the remainder to the act.

» *Start times and performance length*

Be sure that the start time and the length of performance is in line with the performer's wishes and capabilities. You can't contract for a 2-hour show if the performer has only 45 minutes worth of material.

Also consider the performer's stamina. It's impossible to expect a high energy act to perform for any length of time without a breather, so suggest that a break or intermission be included.

If there are to be multiple performances on the same day, be sure to state the start times and lengths of each.

» *Setting times for roving acts*

If this is a roving performance (rather than a stage act), specify how long the act is to perform each hour. For example, "Act is to perform for 20 minutes every hour from 12N to 5PM". Don't promise too much.

Performing for only twenty minutes every hour may seem like a vacation to most of us, but many acts are absolutely grueling. Try dancing in a fur-covered bear suit and rubber mask on a mid-July day (or even on a mid-September day)! I had one such performer come close to suffering heat prostration in such as situation, and she had to spend her "40 minutes off" in the ladies room pouring cold water over her face.

» *Scheduling rain dates*

For outdoor events, purchasers will sometimes ask for a rain date. This issue raises several problems. First, it means that the act must set aside not one, but two days for a single engagement. If a performer isn't heavily booked, that may be no problem, but if their calendar is full, either it may be impossible to offer alternate dates, or the performer may be reluctant to do so. Nothing much can be done—if an act isn't available, it isn't available. To save the booking, you may be able to offer a substitute act if the engagement must be postponed.

Another problem is compensation. If an act must reserve two days, and pass up other possible bookings for both dates, it seems only fair that some compensation should be offered. To charge double would be too costly a surcharge, so I'd suggest adding 25-50% to the standard fee. (Of course, if the rain date is set for several weeks after the original date, and the show takes place on the earlier date, then it's very possible for the act to procure another job for the unused rain date.)

Rain dates are an inconvenience at best, and a costly option at worst. Fortunately, because of other contingencies, some events can't be rescheduled due to bad weather, so the event is either moved indoors or simply canceled.

» *Special arrangements and agreements ("riders")*

Riders are special conditions or agreements that represent demands or needs unique to an act or a particular gig, and should be discussed while you're on the phone with the client. A speaker at a Country Music Association convention described riders as having one purpose: to eliminate any misunderstanding and to provide the best possible show.

You've probably read about some of the exotic riders demanded by certain rock stars and other celebrities ("Twenty cases of Molson on ice, backstage"), but most riders are far more prosaic. Some examples I've encountered are:

- Publicity photos and other promotional materials: "Five sets of photos and posters to be provided to the purchaser at no additional cost."
- Sound system, lights, stage, and other equipment: "Purchaser shall provide amplifier and speaker sufficient for the audience space, six mikes on stands, one mike on miniboom, and two sound monitors".
- Cancellation provisions: "If event is canceled due to bad weather, no charge shall be assessed the purchaser provided that the purchaser notifies the performer prior to 9AM on the day of the performance. Otherwise, there is a change of 50% of the contracted fee."
- Deposits, if required, and the conditions (if any) under which the deposit will be refunded.
- Special routines, songs, costumes, conditions, etc., which the purchaser has specifically requested, e.g., "Performance shall consist of three large-scale stage illusions"

» *Examples of riders*

One kind of "special" is the situation where the purchaser wants a certain orientation to the act—for instance, he or she wants a "message" on health, or racial equality, or energy conservation, or whatever, to be incorporated into the act. Or perhaps it must promote a company or product. Few acts are geared toward a specific message, but magicians, mimes, ventriloquists, and puppeteers can usually incorporate a message into their performance. Again, this is a place where you can use your creative talents to suggest solutions.

In the case of "big name" acts, such matters as audit rights on the box office (where the act's fee is based on box office receipts), the number of free tickets and back stage passes to be given to the act for family and friends, concession rights (i.e., the selling of T-shirts, tapes, and such, and the "cut" or percentage that goes to the act), provisions regarding the taping or filming of the show ("piracy protection"), food, dressing rooms, etc., are commonly dealt with via riders. The complexity and expense of the demands are usually proportional to the price of the act.

Keep in mind that "everything is relative". One time, a talent buyer was complaining that a rider for country star Willie Nelson required that crab legs and Dom Perignon be made available back stage. A bystander asked the buyer what he had paid for Willie and, upon being quoted a high price, shot back, "Then why are you so upset over having to pay for crab legs?"

Sometimes either the performer or the buyer will have a long list of riders which are standard with them. In that case, rather than laboriously writing or typing the entire text into the contract, you can just refer to it so that it becomes part of the contract, e.g., "Riders include the conditions enumerated in the attachment titled 'Standard Contract Riders, New Jersey State Colleges and Universities', which is to become part of this contract."

» *Last-Minute "Surprises"*

No matter how carefully and vigilantly you ask the right questions, make out the contract and cross the t's and dot the i's, and double check all the details, that's no guarantee there won't be a few unpleasant surprises at the last minute.

One time I'd booked Mr. Slim into a small-town Harvest Festival that was to take place in the high school gym. The purchaser assured us that there was a fine stage, plenty of electrical outlets, and even a nearby stage door to facilitate loading and unloading of equipment –everything he could possibly desire. But when he arrived on the day of the performance, he found that directly in front of the stage was a 30-foot-long table, and working behind that table were a half-dozen ladies industriously frying and selling sausage sandwiches! The "sausage concession" couldn't be moved, so Mr. Slim was forced to do three shows behind those busy ladies and their smelly, greasy smoke screen.

But who would have thought to add a rider stating "No sausage stands are to be erected in front of the stage"?

More on Contracts and Other Necessary Evils

At a Country Music Association convention many years ago, Betty Kaye, a talent agent from Sacramento, CA, emphasized the importance of contracts. "It's getting to the point now that everything must be written down. And we (as talent agents) must adapt to a new reality, and that new reality is to have everything in writing."

At some point, you'll have to set all this information down on paper, to be signed by both you and the purchaser. This, in simple terms, is a contract.

How you handle a contract depends on whether you are issuing your own contract, or whether the buyer insists on using their standard contract form.

» *When You Issue the Contract*

Your "standard contract" (see the appendices for an example) should contain all of the items I've discussed above, plus some legalistic "small print" stating that:

"The performer(s) is/are an independent contractor, not an employee of the purchaser, and has exclusive control over the means, methods, and details of fulfilling his/her/their obligations under this contract (with the exception of minimum and maximum performance times)". Note: This provision exempts the purchaser from having to withhold taxes, FICA, etc., and having to contribute FICA and Workingmen's Compensation payments on behalf of the performer.

"The performer shall not infringe upon any copyright, property right, or patent right, and will indemnify the purchaser against any charges, suits, or damages related to any such infringement." Note: Thus, if a musician plays a copyrighted song for which he has not paid a performance royalty, or dresses up as a trademarked character (e.g., The Lone Ranger, Barney the Dinosaur, or Sesame Street's Big Bird), or sells bootlegged T-shirts, the purchaser will not liable in any actions brought by the owner of the copyright or trademark.

"The purchaser assumes no personal liability for the act". Note: This clause protects the purchaser from being held responsible for any injuries or other damages suffered or caused by the act, unless the purchaser is hiring the act personally instead of on behalf of an organization.

— *Sign on the Dotted Line*

Additionally, the contract must include spaces for the dated signatures of the (1) authorized representative of the purchaser, and (2) the act or the agent. Since I usually make out the contract, I almost always sign it (that is, I sign it on behalf of the performer) and then send it to the purchaser, rather than pass it by the performer first. Doing it this way speeds up the whole process but it does have its attendant risks since it makes me solely responsible for the accuracy of the contract and for fulfilling it.

However, some performers will want to read over the contract and sign it themselves before it goes to the purchaser. In that case, the responsibilities are shared by both you and the act.

— *Include the Performer's Phone Number*

Also be sure to include the phone number at which the act can be reached, in case of cancellation or other last-minute crises. Naturally, this should be a phone where the act can be easily reached on the day of the performance. You won't always be around to take the call, so it's important that the purchaser can call the act directly.

There's a slight risk here. Having the performer's personal phone number makes it possible for a purchaser to call up the act directly next time, cutting you out of the deal. But you can reduce this risk if you explain to your acts that any subsequent repeat engagements are commissionable and you have a good working relationship with them, they'll understand the necessity and fairness of not cutting you out.

— *Deadline for Signing and Returning the Contract*

Finally, the contract must specify the deadline for the purchaser's return of the signed contract to you. If the performance date is within the next two months, I usually allow the purchaser 14 days to sign and return the contract. If it's more than two months', I allow at least 14 days or until the end of the current month, whichever is longer.

— *Distributing the Copies*

After you've typed out the contract, sign it, and make three additional copies and distribute them as follows:

- Original contract and copy #1
  Mail both of these to the purchaser, along with any publicity materials you've promised. Mark the Original Contract "KEEP THIS COPY", and mark Copy #1 "PLEASE COMPLETE, SIGN, AND RETURN THIS COPY NO LATER THAN date". If you require additional information from the purchaser (such as a map or directions to the performance site), mark it (use a yellow highlighter pen, or draw arrows).

- Copy #2 of the contract
  Mail this copy to the performer, marked "FOR YOUR FILES". Generally, I don't require the performer to sign and return their copy, but you might decide to have them do so, just to protect yourself.

- Copy #3 of the contract
  Keep this copy for your records until you've received back the signed copy from the purchaser; then you can throw it away and replace it with the signed copy.

— *Adding the Date to Your Business Calendar*

To keep all your bookings straight, you must have some sort of calendar. This can be a large-sized wall calendar, or a desk calendar with sufficiently large spaces to hold the essential booking information, or a computer-based calendar. As soon as you send off a contract, write (in the block for the day of the performance):

- The name of the performer/act
- The name and affiliation of the purchaser
- The time and location
- The fee and commission
- The date the contract was sent and the return deadline.

When you receive back the signed contract, place a green or blue dot and the current date in the block to signify that all the paperwork has been completed.

Check this calendar daily, to make sure that contracts have been returned, and all last-minute details have been taken care of. Also (after the performance) that the fee has been received, and the performer (and you) have been paid.

You'll also use this calendar to remind you to call the performer a day or two before the performance just to make sure that they'll remember to show up (see Chapter 6).

» *When the Purchaser Issues the Contract*

So far in this discussion, we've assumed that *you* are issuing the contract. If the purchaser wants to use their own contract form instead, then do the following:

- Write down the date on your calendar (see above), including the same information as described previously.
- Scan the calendar daily to catch any contracts you've been promised but haven't received.
- Double-check all the information in the contract once you've received it. You may be the type of person who gets everything right the first time, but it's dangerous to assume that everyone works that way.

One of my most devastating and embarrassing experiences involved a summertime engagement several years ago. After discussing several possible dates with the purchaser, we decided on one. The purchaser in this case issued the contract and sent it to me. Alas, both I and the performer failed to notice that the performance date set in the contract was *two months earlier* than the date we had agreed to (it wasn't even one of the dates we had discussed!). As you can guess, the contract date came and went, and I received a rather distressed call from the purchaser the next day. The price we had to pay included not only a $150 fine (as provided in the contract), but also a headlined article (complete with a photo showing the hundreds of people gathered around an empty stage waiting for my "no-show" performer) appeared in a regional newspaper! And it didn't end there. For the next several days I received calls from some of my other clients who, having read the article, wanted to know if they should be concerned about their bookings through my agency. Rest assured, that lesson taught me to look at the date on a contract as soon as I open the envelope.

— *Clauses you may find in client-written contracts*

You'll find that contracts issued by a purchaser tend to be a lot heftier than your 2-page version. Some run to 3, 4 or even 5 or 6 typewritten pages (see Appendix B for an example of a college/school contract). Among the additional provisions you're apt to find are:

- Penalty clauses covering non-performance and other breaches of contract.
- Liability clauses covering injuries to the performer and/or the audience, damage or loss to the performer's equipment, and the like.
- Contingency clauses for canceled performances, rain dates, etc.

The purchaser should provide you with **two** copies of the contract, one to keep, and one to sign and send back before the deadline. Once you've received your signed copy from the client, make an additional copy, and send it to the performer. Mark the calendar with a green or blue dot and the current date to indicate that you've returned the contract to the client.

Invoicing

In addition to the contract, some clients will require an invoice from you before they can issue the check. It's a good idea to always ask your clients if they need an invoice, as they will sometimes forget to ask for it, and this omission can hold up payment later. Use a standard invoice form (available at your local stationery store), and:

- Rubber-stamp or type your name and address at the top.
- Fill in the date of the performance, the name of the act, and the fee.
- Optionally, add a phrase such as "NET 30" (or whatever terms you desire) to the bottom of the form.

Be sure to ask the client to what person or department the invoice should be addressed; it may not always be the person who arranged the entertainment.

Chapter 6
Countdown & Follow-up

In this Chapter:

I've devoted a separate chapter to these two topics, Countdown and Follow-up, not because I have so much material to cover, but because they're so extremely important to your continuing success.

At this point, you've dazzled your client with your sales pitch, sold them the goods, sent out a contract, and assured them that they've made the best of all possible choices.

NOW IT'S TIME TO DELIVER! And how well you deliver depends on how carefully you tie all the loose ends together and keep the client updated on any late breaking developments during this "countdown" period—those last few weeks and days before the big event. You are the vital link between customer and performer, and all the apples are in your basket. If anything goes wrong now, guess who'll get the blame?

But even if everything goes smoothly, your work still isn't over. Once the engagement has passed, you must continue the momentum by following up: Was everyone satisfied? Did everyone pay (or get paid, as the case may be). Are there other opportunities to work with the client again, in the future? This is the time when you can get valuable feedback—valuable because it helps you judge not only your performers, but yourself too.

Count-Down: Those Last-Minute Details

As the date approaches, there are some things you can do:

- Make sure you have the contract in hand, properly signed by the purchaser. If there are any unresolved questions or "fuzzy" areas, now's the time to straighten then out.
- Resolve any "loose ends" at least a week before the performance. For example, if there's any question about the performance being canceled or the performer not being available.
- Mail out your publicity materials, if you've been asked to supply them, and phone the purchaser a few days later, to make sure they've been received.

On the day before a scheduled performance:

- Call both the purchaser and the performer to make sure everything is still A-OK.
- Review with the purchaser the start time of the performance and any props or equipment (lighting, sound system, stage, etc.) the purchaser has agreed to supply.
- Also remind the purchaser of the method of payment agreed to, and confirm that payment will be received as promised (particularly if the performer is counting on receiving a check following the performance to help pay his or her expenses on the way back). It's extremely important to do this (a) when you're dealing with a first-time client, (b) when you're dealing with a new performer, and (c) when you're new at the game yourself.
- Review with the performer the directions to the site, the person he or she is supposed to ask for, and the time of arrival.

» *5 Signs of Trouble*

There are several omens that may indicate that all is not right and you must be alert to them:

- Unreturned contracts
- Ominous rumors about the client or performer
- Murmurs of dissatisfaction from the client
- Novice performers, especially those who don't seem to "have it all together"
- Performers who lack reliable transportation

» *Questionable Bookings*

Clients won't tell you when an event is in trouble. After all, who wants to admit that they couldn't get sufficient support or funding, that they've lost some key players, that their organization is teetering on the brink of insolvency, or that ticket sales are far slower than anticipated? Nope, they'll just hold on to the contract and make feeble excuses as to why they haven't gotten around to signing and returning it to you, and then dump the bad news on you at the last moment.

I had this happen to me twice in one year. In one case, a festival had booked one of my acts for the Fourth of July weekend. The deadline for returning the contract passed, and I started checking with them weekly, and my contact assured me that the "contract is in my purse and I just keep forgetting to mail it." Finally, three days before the performance, they confessed that the festival was in jeopardy. A day later, the Festival was on again, and the next day it was canceled. The result was a performer who had passed up several other offers and now had nothing, on one of the busiest weekends of the year.

In the other instance, I found out via the grapevine that a theater which had not returned a contract was on the verge of bankruptcy. I immediately contacted them, they admitted to the truth of the rumor, and we tore up the contract.

Be firm, and don't let deadlines slip by. If you must, give the client an ultimatum—return the contract within two or three days, or consider the contract canceled.

» *Problem Performers*

On the other side of the coin, some performers (luckily, very few) may prove equally undependable. Keep your ear to the ground and try to pick up any gossip that a performer may have missed a gig, or given an unsatisfactory performance recently.

Also confirm that the performer has reliable transportation to get to the performance site (and backup transportation just in case).Over time, I've dealt with performers who (sans car) were going to "hitch" to the gig, and were still standing by the side of the road when show time came.

Is the performer new? They may get "cold feet" at the last minute, so be sure to give them all the encouragement you can. Illnesses, car breakdowns, and other "acts of God" are unavoidable, but make sure that the performer contacts you (or the client if they can't reach you) immediately, and try to have some sort of backup ready in the wings.

Falling Down on Following Up

An engagement has come and gone, and you've paid the performer and pocketed your commission. Does that mean that you wait until next year before you contact that client again? No—not if you want your business to grow, you don't.

Now is the time to take advantage of the momentum you've started and keep the ball rolling! So, within a week after the performance,

- Call the performer first, to find out if everything went OK. You should try to do this immediately, certainly no later than a day or two after the show, because if anything went wrong you want to know about it as soon as possible so that you can start on damage control.
- Next, call the purchaser, and ask him or her for an evaluation of the performance, and what went right and what (if anything) went wrong. Jot down any good quotes for future use. (Alternatively, you might consider working up an evaluation form to give to purchasers so they can put their comments down on paper.) If the report is favorable, ask for future business (see "Asking for Additional Business" below). If the report is unfavorable, deal with the problem (see "Fielding Complaints" below).
- Send a thank-you card to the purchaser, either shortly after the performance or at the end of the year to thank them for their business.

» *Asking for Additional Business*

Assuming that everything went well, ask the purchaser what's coming up in the near future and if you might be of assistance.

Also ask if they know anyone else who might be in the market for talent. If the answer is "yes", get the necessary information and when you call them, tell them you were referred to them by a satisfied customer.

At the end of the conversation, thank them again for the business, and say, "I'll give you a call around (date) to talk about your (upcoming event)."

» *Fielding Complaints*

If the purchaser has a gripe, listen politely and sympathetically. Sometimes people expect the world for a pittance, but many times the complaints are valid. If they claim that your performer did (or didn't do) something, don't rush to agree, but tell them you'll check with the performer to get his or her story, and then get back to them.

If it turns out that your side is at fault, you may want to adjust the fee for the sake of good will. Being badmouthed throughout the community is not worth the money it might cost to set things right. If you feel that the performer is at fault and should bear a portion of this, discuss it with them. Most importantly, don't be afraid to go back to the client again, after the dust has settled–the worst mistake is to assume that the client will never do business with you again. People understand that performances vary in quality, and that not every act is going to be perfect.

Everyone makes mistakes—it's how you handle those mistakes that determines your success or failure.

Follow-up is one of your most important tasks. When you've done a good job, milk it for all its worth. When you've goofed, settle the account as equitably as possible, resolve never to repeat the mistake, and then go on. "No use crying over spilt milk" applies to the entertainment business as much as to anything else in life.

Chapter 7
It's All Up From Here:
More Opportunities for Growth

One of the really great things about this business is that once you've built a sound foundation, you can expand into any of a dozen or more different directions! After you've been exposed to the myriad facets of this business, you may find yourself drawn to one particular area—perhaps managing, or recording, or promoting, or writing. That doesn't mean you have to drop everything else, but you may find that developing a new interest makes the whole business more exciting and satisfying. At the very least, it's a sure antidote to boredom.

This chapter is not intended to give you an in-depth course on how to do any of these things. I simply want to make you aware of the possibilities and point you in the right direction. Just a few of the avenues you might consider:

- Managing an Act
- Producing Radio/TV Programs
- Hosting Old-time Variety and Vaudeville Shows
- Promoting Concerts
- Producing Albums
- Establishing a Modeling Agency
- Starting a Hollywood-style Casting Agency
- Writing Articles or Books
- Other Diversions

But before you jump into any of these ventures, first make sure you've firmly established your agency business and that things are going smoothly. You don't want to divert your energies at the expense of your major source of income. "Over-expansion" can be fatal!

"Stick With Me, Baby, and I'll Make You a Star!" (Talent Management)

As a "talent booking agent", you're only one of several people in a performer's entourage. A professional act may also have a personal manager, a publicity agent, a business manager, an attorney, "sound" and "light" men, and roadies.

For small acts, you may find yourself filling all these slots, but as you grow into handling larger and more established acts (or, hopefully, as some of the acts you're currently handling grow larger), you'll find that some or all of these people may be needed.

And, at some point, you may elect to switch roles, and take on new responsibilities. One possibility is the role of personal manager.

» *Personal Management*

Becoming a personal manager might be a natural step for you to consider. Personal managing is essentially the job of packaging an act and determining its direction. It's an awesome responsibility and not one to be taken lightly. The talent is putting its entire career in your hands, and they're going to expect a lot more from you than just getting them a few gigs.

For example, let's say you decide to manage a show band. Your duties will vary according to the size and stature of the band and how many other people are on the team.. Among other things, you'll have to decide what outfits they should wear, what types of clubs they should be booked into, what repertoire they should play, and what image they should project. You may have a say in the hiring and firing of the group's members, roadies, and other personnel, as well as their salary and other compensation. You may also shoulder the responsibility for supervising the road crew and other help, purchasing and maintaining the equipment (instruments, sound and light systems, and truck), making hotel and transportation arrangements when they're on the road, and so forth. And, unless the group is big enough to justify a publicity agent, you'll be in charge of producing their press kits, seeing to it that their appearances are properly mentioned in the media, and getting them guest shots on radio and TV. You may have to attend most, if not all, rehearsals and performances, and travel with them on tour.

As you can see, managing is easily a full-time job and, if you choose to do it, you may want to drop your other affiliations and concentrate all your efforts on it.

» *Compensation*

Your compensation would probably be a base salary (ah, a steady income at last!), plus any commissions. But remember—you'll now have all your eggs in one basket, so look before you leap!

Watch Out, Jay Leno, Here I Come (Radio/TV/Web Programming)

TV and radio programming has always fascinated me, and one of my long-time fantasies was to produce (and perhaps even host) my own show.

One day I realized that the variety of acts I represented and the people I knew would provide me with enough interesting guests for a year or more. And I knew that not only would I get great satisfaction from doing it, but I'd essentially have a local version of the Ed Sullivan show on which to present my performers.

The opportunities for getting "on the air" have increased exponentially since cable TV, podcasts, webcasts, and other new media have come along. With forecasts of some day having 500 different channels to choose from, it's obvious that a lot of "product" (programs) will be needed.

Getting your program on the air involves certain basic steps. The descriptions below apply mainly to TV programming, but they are relevant to radio and webcasts as well

» *Scouting the Market*

First, become familiar with the outlets in your area, especially the college-based radio stations, small over-the-air TV stations, and cable television public access channels. Get a program listing for each one, and determine what programs they carry and whether your idea would fit in.

Radio stations revolve around a specific format—news, talk, sports, religion, ethnic cultures, or a specific kind of music (soft rock / easy listening, heavy metal, classical, etc.) UHF stations have a limited broadcast range, but do sometimes produce local shows at relatively inexpensive rates. Cable TV's public access channels usually carry only programs that relate in some way to the community in which they're located, although some of them will carry any programming that's deemed to be of general interest.

» *Writing a Proposal*

Next draw up a proposal. This should include the name of your program, its theme and format, examples of the kinds of guests you plan to have on the show, and an estimated budget. List the major participants (producer, director, host, and other staff) and state their qualifications. It should also discuss, in the strongest possible terms, why you think the program would appeal to the station's audience.

» *Selecting Your Staff*

Select a host (yourself or someone else), a producer (probably you), and a director. At some of the smaller radio stations, you may also have to supply an engineer (the person who operates the control panel, assures that the transmitted signal is up to standard, etc.). And on cable TV, you'll have to supply your own camera crew, floor director, and video editors. Fortunately, most cable outlets offer free courses for training these people.

Of all these, the host is the most important. A complete amateur just won't cut it, so get someone with acting experience.

If you have colleges in your area that offer Theater or Communications courses, you may be able to recruit students to serve as interns in some of these positions (an intern is a student or recent graduate who agrees to work gratis on your show in return for course credits or experience).

» *Pitching Your Concept*

Once you have your proposal together, make an appointment with the station manager. If he or she shows interest and is willing to give your program a trial run, you may, depending on the type of station, have to come up with sponsors (advertisers) to underwrite the expense. Otherwise, you may have to fund the show yourself. (This does not apply to cable TV public access channels, which are free to community residents.)

Some stations are non-profit and don't carry advertising. Other stations have a set hourly charge for air time (and, in the case of TV stations, for studio and editing time), and carry ads sold either through their own sales staff or brought in by you.

» *Doing a Pilot*

Assuming that everything can be agreed to, the station may ask you to do a pilot show, for which you might have to put up the money.

For example, to do a half-hour talk show on a small, local UHF station in Boston back in the 1980s cost me $600 ($300 for studio time, and $300 for air time) We shot it "on the fly", but if we'd had to do any tape editing afterwards, that would have been additional. Be sure you have a clear idea of what it's going to cost you before you start, and get it in writing.

After you've finished the pilot, the station management will review it to determine if it meets their standards and needs. If it does, and you're willing to proceed, the station will probably offer you a short-term contract (usually three months). If there are costs involved, you will be responsible for them, although you (or the station) may find advertisers to provide the money.

» *A Typical Scenario*

Let me tell you a bit about my own experiences. Some time back, I decided to produce a half-hour program, *Boston Showcase*, on a UHF channel here in Boston. Appointing myself as executive producer, I recruited a staff of four student interns from Boston University's School of Public Communication: a producer, a director, an assistant director, and a program host.

We spent several months planning the format of the show and putting together a pilot, which consisted of three segments: the first on a local street singer, the second on a street magician, and the third on past-life regression. Deducting time for station breaks and commercials, that means 22 actual minutes (or less) of program time, or three 7-minute segments. We did the show, it met approval, and it aired a number of times. Unfortunately, we were unable to come up with the number of sponsors needed, so the show eventually died.

Later, I resurrected the program with a new team and new name (*The Jane Harman Show*, after the hostess) and did a new pilot, this time on one of the nation's best known UFO abductees, Betty Hill. Then we did a second pilot, featuring boxing champ "Marvelous Marvin" Haggler, and laid out a schedule of future programs. This series, too, eventually folded due to the lack of sustained revenue.

Finally, I approached Continental Cablevision, which had a number of local cable outlets in the area, and proposed doing a new series, *Personal Perspectives*, a weekly series of half-hour programs spotlighting unusual people, occupations, beliefs, and talents. I supplied the production and the host, while the station provided all of the technical backup, including camera crew and editing technicians. We featured hypnotists, UFO believers, witches, sword-swallowers, computer gurus, strippers, and all manner of weird and wonderful guests, and it was so successful it ran for almost six years.

After the first year of *Personal Perspectives*, I added a second weekly program series, *SexStyles*, which dealt with relationships and human sexuality. I sometimes jokingly referred to it as "Boston's version of Dr. Ruth". Admittedly, it was a harder sell, due to it being so controversial, but I finally got the go-ahead, and it ran for almost four years. Besides being broadcast from the outlet where we did the taping, we distributed it to many of Continental's other outlets and to the independent cable outlets in Boston and Cambridge.

An offshoot of cable TV production is videotape production and distribution. In my case, I've had the tapes from my cable series listed in various DVD and videotape catalogs as educational programs, and have received more than a few orders for them. And a DVD/videotape, like an audio cassette, has a number of uses; besides being a marketable product, it's a handy tool for auditions and for exhibiting at your trade show booth.

Also, I've worked with some friends of mine, who own and operate Vivid Image Productions, in making a series of videotapes about ghosts and hauntings. My associates traveled over to England and Scotland with ghost hunters Ed and Lorraine Warren, videotaping many of the haunted sites for which the British Isles are famous, and we put these episodes together under the title, *Journey Beyond*. I wrote the script, and Don Westcott of NOVA was the narrator. Subsequent tapes are slated to focus on such topics as angels, demonic possession, and UFOs. Although the tapes are mainly intended for retail sales, we have a number of PBS television outlets interested in airing them and it's entirely possible that this could lead to a television series.

Producing Your Own Variety Stage Show (Producing Vaudeville-style Theater)

Vaudeville Lives! Earlier in this book I talked about the time I put together a talent showcase for a group of parks and recreation directors. You might consider expanding on this idea and packaging an old-time vaudeville review (complete with free dinner dishes, if you want to be truly authentic), an *Ed Sullivan* variety show, a musical revue, a circus, or whatever extravaganza you can dream up.

With the nostalgia craze that's been going on for the past decade, with its "50s Rock-n-Roll Shows", such an idea could be a big hit! And you probably have the acts already in your back pocket.

In my area, a number of old-time movie theater houses have been restored and they're offering these types of 'live' shows with some success. Some of these theaters still have their original theater organs, oil-painted backdrops, and other props from those bygone days, and I find that it's a lot of fun to work them into the program.

To bring back these Good Old Days, you'll have to:

- Check the town laws concerning public events and get the necessary OKs. You may need a special entertainment permit, on-duty police officers for crowd control and security, and a bond and other liability coverage.
- Rent (or otherwise obtain) an auditorium, theater or outdoor arena in which to hold your show. Or you might strike up a deal with a restaurant or club owner to let you produce a show as dinner theater or cabaret entertainment for their patrons.
- Arrange for a sound system staging, lighting, and other equipment unless the facility can provide them.
- Choose three or four acts and put together a program. The idea of vaudeville is something for everyone, so create a good mix—a musical act, a magic act, perhaps a comedian, and a novelty act (juggler, acrobat, trained animals, and the like).
- Set a modest admission charge (today anything under $20 is considered to be "modest") and print up a supply of tickets.

- Publicize your show by blanketing the area with posters, mailing press releases to the local media, and spreading the news by word-of-mouth.
- Mail special invitations to high-ranking prospects (the mayor, city council, school committee, etc.), and enclose complimentary tickets.
- Consider providing a refreshment stand serving light refreshment at intermission.
- Arrange for a literature table with brochures or 1-sheeters on the acts performing in the show.
- Recruit ticket sellers and ticket takers, ushers, stage hands, and any other help you'll need.

If you're producing the show in conjunction with a club, restaurant, or other organization (you might sell the idea of putting on the show as a fund-raiser), work out an arrangement where they pay you either a flat fee or a minimum guarantee plus a percentage of the proceeds. Remember: you have to give your performers something, and pay all the expenses, too. At least until you're established, it's best to split your income with the acts prorata.

If your efforts bring success, you may want to continue the shows on a regular basis, say once a month. After you're better able to estimate the gate, you might want to switch to a flat fee for each performer.

How Much to Rent the Astrodome? (Concert Promotion)

Concert promotion is somewhat akin to producing a variety show, only on a larger scale. If you're representing one or more popular musical acts, this may be a way to get them exposure and make money at the same time.

The process for doing this is much like that for putting together a variety or vaudeville revue, except that it's more complex due to the size of the undertaking and— particularly if you're planning on doing rock or heavy metal concerts— you're going to have a few more barriers to overcome. Because concerts are usually large scale events, they offer a better chance to make a real killing, but they also offer a better chance to get burned.

If you're serious about concert promotion, I urge you to apprentice yourself to a seasoned promoter first, just to learn the ropes. Or you might become an in-house booking agent for a local night club. In either case, offer your services for a modest price, because the education, experience, and contacts will be worth many times your paycheck.

If and when you decide to break away on your own, arrange to pay for the talent and site on a percentage (or base plus percentage) of gross revenues. You'll have less chance of losing your shirt that way. You're talking a lot of money here, so get some good legal advice, and have all contracts approved by your attorney; one slip-up could ruin you financially for life. This is one venture when it makes good sense to set up a corporation to protect your personal assets, should something go horribly wrong. And, along with a good lawyer, be sure to have a good accountant.

As with any venture in this chapter, I'd suggest starting at the low end and working your way up. Generally, you'll want to position your ticket prices somewhere between those of local coffeehouses and nightclubs, and the "name" concerts, so we're talking about acts that can draw a crowd at $15-30 a head. Look for up-and-coming bands that have built up a strong local following and are headed for the Big Time (easier said than done, because if you should be lucky enough to discover such a group, there'll probably be some other promoter who already has them sewn up).

But who knows—if you have that rare talent for spotting a future headliner that everyone else is ignoring, and you happen to be in the right place at the right time, you might discover the next Bruce Springsteen.

As for me, I've put on a number of holiday folk concerts. My budget has always been minimal. We rent a large church right in downtown Boston. We do all our own mailing, posters, promotions. And we serve apple cider and cookies at intermission. Ticket prices average around $15-25, and we sell albums and other souvenirs. We'll never get rich at this, but we've managed to do a bit better than break even. And the non-monetary benefits (exposure, strengthening the "fan club", getting wider distribution for the cassettes and CDs) are definitely worth the effort. Plus we always get a few reviewers from the local papers to attend. The concerts have become a Boston Tradition, and that's something not to be trifled with!

At the Top of the Charts (Album Producing)

Record producer - I'm covering this subject in greater detail than the others, for two reasons. First, it's something that you're very likely to do at some point, especially if you handle musical acts (which probably accounts for most of you). And secondly, it's something with which I've had a good deal of experience.

When I started in 1975, everything was on vinyl records, 8-tracks were just starting to come in, and cassettes and CDs weren't even thought of, but times have changed. Producing a CD for one of your bands or other musical acts offers a number of advantages. For example, it can:

- Give the fans something to take home as a souvenir after a concert.
- Serve as an excellent promotion and audition tool.
- Help finance other ventures.
- Reach other artists who might want to perform some of your artist's original songs
- Establish the artist as "serious" ("Wow, they've even got a CD out!").

If you represent many musical acts, you'll soon get tired of burning CDs, packaging and labeling them, and mailing them out to radio stations, prospective buyers, and others. And you'll get even more tired having to pay for them.

» *How to "Break Even" on an Album*

Let me make one point very clear: in most cases your goal in making an album is to promote the group, *not to make money*. Unless you're a big label (and even they have their duds), you're not going to make a cash profit on this. BUT, if your group has a sufficient following, producing a CD will almost always cover your expenses, even if you sell only half of them! So, if you make 600 copies, and you sell 300, you'll have the remaining 300 for free, to send out in press kits, to radio stations, and for auditioning. The only trick is to budget your costs so that they don't exceed the total gross selling price of one-half the number of tapes or CDs you plan to produce.

Basically, you'll need a minimum of $2500-3000 to start. If you're a bit short of cash, consider offering a pre-publication special, giving a discount or some other incentive to those fans who order and pay for the album in advance. Then you can put that money toward the production. Let's factor the figures and see how they work:

Production costs for recording and duping <u>600</u> copies	$3,000.00
Receipts from gross sales of <u>300</u> copies at $10 each	- 3,000.00
Net Cost $0.00	

And you'll have the remaining 300 copies for free!

» What About "Singles"?

Don't do "singles"—they may cost less, but they offer proportionately less in return. With a single, you're presenting only a narrow sampling of an artist's songs, while on a full CD you can squeeze in 10 to 12 songs and demonstrate the full spectrum of their talents and abilities.

But even more important, singles (even those of top-name artists) simply don't sell as well as albums. The reason is obvious: an album offers a much better value to the buyer, too. (But if you really want to buy 800 singles, cheap, just give me a minute; I have some down in my basement.)

» Getting Started

Alright, let's assume you have a promising artist or group, and you're raring to capture them on Memorex. What do you need, what steps do you have to go through to get it, and how much will it cost?

» Obtaining Mechanical Rights

Most times, an album will mainly consist of original compositions written by members of the group. But if your group plans to record another artist's material, you first have to obtain mechanical rights to that material, that is, the right to record the song. Since a common practice is to include several songs made popular by another group (sometimes referred to as "cover" songs) in an album to enhance its appeal, it's likely that you'll have to obtain mechanical rights for at least one of the numbers.

In the old days, you would have had to track down the songwriter personally, beg them for permission to use a song (permission which the songwriter may decide to refuse), and negotiate the fee to be paid in return. Today, the process is much easier. The government copyright laws decree that a songwriter who has allowed a work to be recorded once must grant the same rights of recording to anyone else for a standard royalty fee. Furthermore, an entity known as The Harry Fox Agency in the Big Apple handles the granting of these rights for almost all the songwriters. If you've decided to use someone's song, you fill out a license application for the song, and send along a nominal sum; this money goes, in part, to the songwriter as a royalty fee.

Note: Don't confuse The Harry Fox Agency with ASCAP or BMI (see Chapter 2). The latter two organizations handle performance rights and collect royalties for public performances of a musical work.

Using the example above, if one of the songs you're recording belongs to someone else and you're duping 600 copies, you'd owe a small royalty, not anything that will break the bank.

» *Recording the Album*

You can record either in a recording studio or at a live performance (doing it at a dead performance is not generally recommended). That's a joke... Arguments for recording *in the studio* include:

- A more controlled atmosphere, with better acoustics and free from the irritating chatter, coughing, babies crying, and other noises of an audience.
- A better chance to listen to each piece and redo it if necessary (tens or even dozens of times, if need be).
- Better equipment, relatively speaking, for the price.

Arguments for recording a *live performance* include:

- Some groups, needing audience feedback to encourage them, do their best in front of a live audience
- The performance doubles as a recording session (sort of a "killing two birds with one stone")
- A special kind of ambiance (not to mention enthusiastic applause) can be obtained only in a performance setting.

On the negative side, a remote (outside the studio) session may be more expensive, since the recording engineer had to truck his equipment to the performance, set it up, and later knock it down and repack it. Also, a remote session may not produce as clean and professional results as could be obtained in a professional studio.

» *Flavors of Recording*

Recording comes with a variety of options, and the ones you pick determine the price. There are 4-track, 8-track, 16-track, and 32-track (do you sense a pattern here?) studios. The more tracks, the more money. Mostly, the number of tracks is determined by the number of musicians in the group–if you can afford to do so, miking each person and recording him or her on a separate track gives you much more latitude later during editing. Then there are the "extras" like special effects, synthesizers, and other special equipment. Most studios insist that you use one of their recording engineers, but sometimes you can supply your own.

» *Saving Money*

Given the above, you might think that the way to cut costs is to reduce the number of tracks. But that can be penny wise and pound foolish, and cause problems later, like when you're mixing (editing) and trying to balance the drums vis-à-vis the guitar and vocals. Better ways to save money in the recording studio include:

- Buying time in blocks (there are 8-, 16, and 24-hour blocks). It's cheaper than buying it by the hour.
- Choosing off-time blocks rather than prime time. Since most people in the music business are night people and have unconventional lifestyles, you won't pay more for recording on 2nd or 3rd shift or even weekends, in fact you'll probably save money.

- Being rehearsed and prepared, and knowing exactly what you want to do. Most of the time and money wasted in a recording session is due to not being prepared. Know what songs you want to record, what instruments you're going to use, and who is going to do what and when. Then rehearse, rehearse, and rehearse, before you get to the studio and the meter starts running.

» *Editing*

Once you've got all your stuff "laid down", the next step is editing.   Editing is always done in the studio, where sophisticated equipment allows you to balance the various tracks and "mix" all 8 or 16 or whatever tracks down to two tracks (since most playback systems are stereo). For example, you can soften the drums on one track so they don't drown out the vocals on another track. You can also make corrections to a track (cut out a pause, a noise, or other glitch), apply special effects such as echo or reverberation, and patch in sound effects such as applause. Then "gaps" must be added at the beginning and end of the tape (to allow for the clear "leader") and between the songs. The end result is known as a master.

To do this, you need an engineer who specialized in editing. Editing costs are equal to or higher than recording charges, so if you do it right in the first place (i.e., when you're recording), you can save a bundle at the other end.

When I first started producing albums (again, we're talking 33-and-1/3 RPM vinyl here, not CDs), it was a very crude, laborious process. Since there was no sophisticated editing equipment in those days, everything was done by hand, literally. For example, if a vocalist mispronounced a word in the middle of the song, the engineer would have to play back the master tape to that point, manually rock the tape back and forth over the playback head to find the exact spot, physically cut out the section of tape containing the offending phrase with a razor blade, and patch in the piece of tape containing the correction. One of the engineers we used lived on Beacon Hill, and we worked out of his apartment, the same place and the same equipment he used when editing Joan Baez's first album, and he was truly such a master at his art that he could surgically excise a single breath if you wanted him to!

» *Production*

The final stage of this process is the production phase, and consists of several steps: duping the master tape onto CDs, printing and affixing labels, printing, folding, and inserting the jackets into the plastic cases, and putting all the pieces together and shrink-wrapping them. You can choose to do all this at a one-stop shop, or you can have each step performed by a separate company. The one-stop approach is cheaper and easier, but the other way gives you more control.

As an aside, in the "old days" of vinyl records, production was a lot more complicated and expensive. First, you had to send your tape to a mastering company, which played it into a cutting machine to make a *mother recording*, a solid Bakelite platter that resembled a phonograph record, but was actually a mirror image (with all the bumps and grooves reversed). Then the "mother" was used to make a metal disk, called the *master pressing*, from which each vinyl copy was pressed. If you wanted to check the results before the final manufacture, you had to ask them to send you a *reference copy*. If there was anything wrong, you had to go back to square one and start over. All in all, the process took weeks and was much more expensive than today's approach.

» *Duping*

Today, it's a much simpler, one-step process. When you send your master tape to a production company, they place it on a master playback unit, which records it onto the individual blank CDs mounted on a network of recording units.

» *Labeling*

Labels must be designed and printed on both sides of the CD case. The production company can provide you with a choice of standard labels, or you can have someone design a label for you and provide it to the production house.

» *Jackets*

This is the printed cover that lines the plastic outer case for the CD. Either you can supply a rough sketch along with the text to the production company and let them do the final design and printing, or you can do your own design and have them produced by an outside printer. Generally, a jacket consists of photo of the group and title on the front, song titles on the back, and descriptive text (which can include a word sheet for all the songs) on the inside.

» *Assembling*

All these pieces have to be brought together and assembled, and then the entire package is shrink-wrapped and packed in cartons for shipping. The next day or so, the cartons arrive at your doorstep and you're ready to go out and peddle them. And that brings us to the next topic.

» *Distribution*

Now that you have that stack of boxes occupying half your living room, what do you do with them? Here are a few suggestions:

- Sell them at intermission and after each performance. Be sure to announce their availability during the performance, and provide an easily seen table display near the entrance.
- Place them on consignment in as many local record stores as possible.
- Run small ads in appropriate publications.
- Set up a booth at gatherings, such as folk festivals, fairs, battle-of-the-bands contests, and other relevant spots.
- Use word-of-mouth to promote the album.

If you've produced a couple thousand, you may be able to interest some small local distributor in carrying it. But remember that you won't receive full retail for any CD you don't sell directly; you'll have to wholesale to the record stores at 40% off the retail price, and to distributors at 60% off.

» *The Balance Sheet*

So what does all this add up to? Well, take your total costs, and divide them by the number of copies you've made, and there's your unit cost. If your aim is to have 'free' copies to distribute for promotional purposes, double that figure and sell half of them at that price, leaving you with half for your own use. Or sell them all, and make a profit.

The World of Dior: Models for All Occasions (Running a Modeling Agency)

Another natural outgrowth of a talent agency is a **modeling agency**. Here in Boston, there are several such agencies that combine both services under one roof.

In essence, both types of agencies operate very similarly, because there's little difference between hiring out an attractive model to staff a trade show booth or a clown to bring in customers to a grand opening. In fact, some of my performers, actors, and actresses are also available as models should the opportunity arise.

All of which makes sense, since most performers are attractive, some even charismatic, and are certainly adept at working in front of audiences and cameras. Look over your own roster –I'm sure you'll find that some of your performers, given the right makeup and clothes, could rival many of the models you've seen in the ads. Look for any training or background in acting; people who know how to present themselves on stage usually have no trouble with the average modeling assignment. Acting is also valuable experience in qualifying for "voice-overs" in radio and TV commercials.

Don't assume that "model" refers only to the gorgeous people you see in *Gentlemen's Quarterly* or *Vogue*—there are character models, too, and some of your people may belong in that category. Clowns and mimes frequently appear in ads, both on TV and in print (remember the mime who played Charlie Chaplin in those old ads for IBM personal computers?)

Many times a modeling agency runs several sideline businesses, offering photography services or a modeling school for example.

Or, perhaps, you don't want to run an agency, but instead supply models to already established agencies. One of my friends has a little 7-year-old "Dakota Fanning" look-alike, to whom I'm proud to be an 'adoptive' father, and we've started her on the road to a modeling career.

A Hollywood Casting Agency (Casting for the Movies)

And very close to modeling is **casting**: finding "just the right people" to star in a movie, or appear in a new TV sitcom, or be a guest on a national TV talk show. The good news is that *Hollywood is no longer the center of the movie industry*. Many major cities – Boston, for one – now have film bureaus, and their streets are beginning to look like a Hollywood backlot.

If this possibility interests you, find out if your state has a Film Bureau or some such agency whose primary purpose is to convince the Hollywood studios to film their productions in your neck of the woods. If so, make sure to list yourself with them as a supplier.

Casting directors, like everyone else, look for ways to make their job easier, and if you can prove to them that you can help them find the people they're looking for, they'll be happy to send assignments your way. In the past year or two, I took my stepson to an audition for Paramount's "School Ties" and he was hired for three months' work as an extra, and I was approached by 20th Century Fox to find a "River Phoenix look-alike" for "A Far Country". New England, and the Boston area in particular, is growing as a desirable site for filming movies, and as I write, "The Crucible" is being shot here in Salem, just 20 or so miles away.

Once you've established a working relationship with a casting director at a Hollywood studio, you'll receive periodic "wish lists" from them,. sometimes accompanied by two or three pages of script. Frequently, they'll ask you to have you videotape your candidate(s) acting out this script and send it to them as a preliminary audition.

I used to think that all the actors and actresses I saw on screen were somehow "grown" in a factory in Los Angeles and sent to acting school at age 5, but I've come to realize that Hollywood still looks for new faces, if not on a soda-fountain stool at Schwab's Drugstore, then in hometown America.

Nationally televised talk shows (*Geraldo, Oprah, Maury Provich, Joan Rivers, et al*) are always looking for unusual people to spotlight (and who knows more unusual people than we agents?) I'm sort of an unofficial "scout" for Geraldo, having been his guest at one time myself, and occasionally I get a call from the producer asking if I know of people who are into group marriages or are transvestites, or some such thing. (And strangely enough, more often than not, I do!)

Lectures, Classes, Tours

There are so many ways you can branch out, it would take a book twice this size to adequately cover them. In my own experience, I've given presentations at bookstores, schools, and libraries, I've taught courses at Continuing Adult Education centers, and I've even started a ghost hunting group, *a la* SyFy Channel's *Ghost Hunters*.

» *Lectures*

Libraries, bookstores, schools, and other institutions are always looking for interesting speakers, and with a business like this, you certainly qualify! But be aware that you won't get rich at this— most of these gigs pay only a pittance or sometimes nothing at all. The deal here is publicity, just one more way to get the word out about yourself.

» *Classes*

Almost every metropolitan area today offers adult education courses and you might consider teaching others how to become talent booking agents. What I'd advise is, don't teach too close to home because you don't want to create competition in your own backyard. Instead, choose a large city perhaps 10-20 miles away. For example, I live and work in Waltham, a community about 10 miles outside of Boston, so teaching in Boston or in nearby Cambridge doesn't present a problem for me, as there's plenty of opportunity for everyone.

» *Tours*

This is a bit of a stretch for most of you, but in my situation I've had a lifelong interest in the paranormal, I represent a number of people in that field, and I've founded a ghosthunting group, *Boston Paranormal Investigators*. On a monthly basis we investigate some reportedly haunted site, armed with our instruments, and try to capture evidence of spirits. From this humble beginning, I'm looking into the possibilities of conducting overnight ghost tours, wherein people pay a fee to accompany us and learn the rudiments of ghost hunting. Other possible extensions include offering walking tours of sites associated with mysteries, hauntings, and other legendary happening.

If ghosts aren't your thing, come up with another focus of which you have specialized knowledge, like a tour of little-known clubs that feature cult bands of a particular genre—grunge, hip-hop, new age jazz, etc. It doesn't have to be just music—how about setting up a behind-the-scenes tour of theaters, magic shows, or circuses?

You've Got a Story to Tell (Book Publishing)

I've put this topic at the end, both because it's not intrinsic to the talent business and because only a few of you are cut out to be writers. But I had to include it because it was *my* particular door into the entertainment world.

Believe it or not, Tom Elliott Productions really grew from a book! Having been an avid fan of street performers for a number of years, I wanted to write a booklet about them.

Somewhere along the way, I met one of the most beloved of the genre, a lovely golden-haired princess named RuthAnna. As she and I worked together on the book (which increasingly focused on her, to the exclusion of all the rest), I became more and more involved with her career: designing leaflets and posters, looking around for places where she could perform, and assisting her in staging folk concerts. Soon word spread to the other street performers, and I began to receive calls asking me if I'd do the same for them. Soon I had 50 to 60 acts on the string before I'd realized what was happening.

You might consider writing a book, too, but as an outgrowth rather than the origin of your business. You're going to be meeting a lot of interesting people, and each one has a unique history and lifestyle. I personally know at least a dozen performers, each of whose lives would make a book! The public is fascinated by people who are offbeat, bizarre, or even (dare I say it) weird. Just look at the sales of magazines like *People*, *Us*, and the tabloid newspapers such as the *National Inquirer* and *Star*. Several books on street entertainers have already appeared and are selling well. My favorite, which I read and greatly enjoyed, is called "Passing the Hat".

If this idea appeals to you, I'd suggest you carry a small mini-tape-recorder with you and record your conversations with performers (with their permission, of course) when you're gathering information about them. Then you'll be ready to turn it on if they should launch into a particularly interesting story. I did this whenever Capt. Don started talking about his days with the old-time circuses, or when Pif began discoursing on her alter ego. If nothing else, I'm preserving a living folk history of show business, told by the people who have experienced it first-hand.

Or, if you don't want to write a book, how about a magazine article or news item? It can be on a subject as well as a person—circus life, the art of pantomime, the different types of clown faces, a history of juggling, or whatever you feel inspired to write about. Your performers, of course, are a great source of material, as many of them have studied their art as well as practiced it.

I do occasional articles myself, and my published efforts have ranged from UFOs to producing cablevision programs.

As I've said many times before, being a talent agent opens the door to a world of infinite possibilities. And your only task is to decide which ones you want to follow up on!

Chapter 8
Some Parting Words...

At this point, the authors of most how-to books say, "OK, I've told you everything I know, you're on your own, good luck and God Bless!"

In one sense, you *are* on your own, because you now have all the information you need to survive by yourself (and a lot more information than *I* had when I started!).

But I know you're going to have a lot of questions and maybe even more than a few problems. And I know it's going to take you a while to assemble a respectable line-up of performers. So, rather than leaving you "lost at sea without a life raft", I'm going to do something few authors do: I'm going to give you my phone number, email address, and mailing address so you can reach me with your questions. .

Before we get to that, I want to tell you about some of the more interesting experiences I've had in my years as a talent agent, because I consider my experiences as the true reward. And without them, I probably would have quit long ago, and I certainly wouldn't have written this book to encourage you to follow in my steps.

Just a Few Anecdotes from over 30 Years in the Business

Since I started back in 1975, I've had so many wonderful and fascinating experiences, that I could fill another book. Entertainment is a world unto itself, and the people in it are not your 9-to-5 office workers. So it should come as no surprise that working with them is anything but ordinary.

» *The Human Volcano*

I've mentioned my sideshow act, the late Capt. Don, a number of times in this book, but I haven't said much about his grand finale—the Human Volcano. (If we were playing *Jeopardy*, the correct response would be, "What's 40 feet long, black and red all over, and explodes like a hundred firecrackers?")

After going through his standard repertoire of fire-eating, sword-swallowing, and other wonders, the Captain's grand finale was what he called The Human Volcano, the explosive eruption of a 40-foot-long black and red flame from his mouth. And the key to doing this is a special "cocktail" that he imbibed just prior to the stunt—consisting of diesel fuel, gun powder, and gasoline!

Since diesel fuel and gunpowder are not something you can buy at the general store, Capt. Don would bring his own supply, but gas is more readily available, if not from a pump then from a nearby car.

So, at many a show, I've gone prowling with him to look for a car from which to siphon a pint or two of gas. When we found one, he took out a length of flexible tubing, inserted it into the fuel inlet, put the other end of the tubing between his lips, drew up a goodly amount of gasoline, then quickly repositioned that end into an old tin can he carried around with him, and let it flow until the can was half full. After he got back to center stage, he added the gun powder and diesel fuel and let it "ferment" until he was ready to use it.

Near the end of his performance, the Captain lit a torch, then picked up the can, filled his mouth with the potent fluid, and then sprayed the concoction out over the flame, producing a 40'-long fire ball that shot straight across the stage with a roar that could be heard in the back row.

Don also performed traditional fire-eating, using up to three lit torches, and one time when I'd booked him for a Town Day festival, he was performing on a rug covered platform, when some of the flaming liquid dribbled down his chin and onto the carpet—Whoosh! Suddenly he was standing in a circle of flames that quickly consumed every fiber of the rug—an added touch to his already fiery finale.

People always ask me if he ever got hurt plying his trade. Luckily, he's never been seriously injured by fire. He had some of his facial hair burned off while doing the Human Volcano, but much worse happened to a fellow fire-eater. One of them was performing on a nightclub stage and, just as he was about to spew the cocktail over the torch, someone at the back of the room turned on the air conditioner, which blew the flame back at the performer. Tragically, the fire ignited the gas fumes that pervaded the poor soul's mouth and lungs, and he literally blew up in full view of the audience.

He suffered several serious injuries from sword-swallowing, however. Once, while performing in a club, he'd just swallowed a sword when a drunk wandered on stage and bumped into him, sending him sprawling while the sword was still inside. He cut himself up pretty badly, but rather than seek medical aid, he managed to reach home and go to sleep ("I figured that if I woke up the next morning, I couldn't be too badly hurt", he said nonchalantly.) Again, one of his fellow performers wasn't so lucky. A student of Don's, having just mastered the art, was in a bar one day. Someone challenged him to swallow a sword and, being somewhat inebriated, he attempted to do so, stumbled and fell, and bled to death before he reached the hospital.

Moral: Sword-swallowing and fire-eating are for the trained professional—DON"T try it at home!

» *Is That Monkey Wearing Pampers?*

Shopping malls have their own set of rules, and I found out that one of those rules is that all animals on the premises must be properly attired. No, I don't mean in tuxes or nifty dog vests or rhinestone-studded cat collars, I mean properly *diapered*.

In their ever vigilant effort to preserve the antiseptic cleanliness of America's Shopping Meccas, many malls won't risk the unsightly spectacle of animals relieving themselves during a public appearance. I first discovered this fact one time when I had booked an organ grinder and monkey act at a posh North Shore mall here in New England. The act and I had just arrived when one of the mall management came up to us and asked us to put a diaper on Jo-Jo the monkey before show time. Despite protests that Jo-Jo wouldn't take kindly to such an affront, the management remained adamant, and so we went off in search of a package of Pampers for Preemies.

Fortunately, everything worked out OK and the show went on, but I've always wondered whether monkeys hold a grudge, because several months later as I was playing with Jo-Jo at another mall, he lunged at me and bit a good-sized piece off my index finger. With thoughts of terminal monkey fever driving me to panic, I ran around the arcade looking for a bottle of hydrogen peroxide, and when I found it, poured half of it into the wound. Assured that Jo-Jo was disease free, I went ahead with my plans to fly off to Jamaica the following day, but for the next week or so I pictured myself being Medvaced from there to the US mainland for treatment of some dread tropical malady.

» *The Almost Traveling Sideshow*

Seven or eight years ago, one of my acts and I decided to build a traveling sideshow and take it on the road.

It was going to be a so-called Ten-in-One in carnival parlance (ten acts under one tent for one admission), and would consist of a Sword-Swallower, Fire-Eater, Human Pincushion (that's someone who sticks pins and needles through his flesh), Human Block Head (the guy who hammers screwdrivers, awls, nails, and other objects up his nostrils and "into his brain"), the Electric Chair (a girl sits in a highly charged chair and zaps key rings and lights up neon tubes), a ZigZag Box (a contortionist act), the Snake Pit Girl (self-explanatory), Magician, Bed of Glass, and one other attraction.

Well … we built it, but it never hit the asphalt. My partner, who would have had to manage the day-to-day operation got cold feet and left me high and dry.

But I learned a lot about sideshows during that time. One amazing fact about sideshows (and you'll know this if you've been to many of them) is that a Ten-in-One can be run by only three or four people! You need one person to do the "geek" (gross-out) acts (swords, fire, pincushion, bed of glass, blockhead), and a young, beautiful lady to do the electric chair, zigzag, and snakepit, and possibly one other to be the magician, master of ceremonies, and anything else that's needed. And you need a ticket-taker for the outside.

The plan was to have my partner do the major acts and pick up people along the road to fill the other positions (the other acts require no special skills and are easily taught). So, essentially what you have is a one-man show masquerading as a 10-person spectacular. Except for the main man, the others will usually stay with the show for one or two weeks, and then they'll get tired of the 12-hour days, collect their paycheck, and disappear.

Several times I flew out to San Francisco, where he was headquartered, and conferred on the various aspects of the show and helped him purchase the necessary equipment. (He was the brains, I was the money.) What a shopping list! First we needed endless yards of canvas for the large hand-painted posters you see out front, the sidewalls of the tent, and the skirts on the platforms inside the tent. Add to this a large fuse box panel, electric cables, and fuses for the various electronics (lights, PA systems), a generator for the electric chair, and a truck to carry it all. I spent several days wiring up the fuse panel, a difficult task since I'd never done electrical work in my life. One day we went to a used car dealer, cash in hand, bought a panel van, and I drove it back to town, almost getting lost on the unfamiliar streets. Later we added a 2-wheel trailer, and my partner built a caboose-like structure on it to use as living quarters while on the road. It looked a bit like a log cabin on wheels.

Meanwhile my partner started painting the canvas posters in the traditional side-show style, showing the various acts that one would view "on the inside". It's a shame he never finished them, as they would be worth a great deal of money to collectors of carnival and circus memorabilia.

At some point during this period, I heard of a circus fat lady who'd broken up with her manager and was available. My partner suggested adding her show to ours, but I didn't want more responsibilities and declined the offer.

One time when I was out on the West Coast, I got a guided tour of the studios of the famed tattoo artists (including the guy who had done Janis Joplin's *Rose*), and one of them—Henry Goldfield—personally designed and inscribed a beautiful Wolf Head tattoo on my upper right arm. As Groucho Marx used to say on *You Bet Your Life* when it came time to guess the "secret word", a tattoo is "something you'll always have with you."

Contrary to popular belief, being tattooed doesn't hurt any more than a pinprick, although I enjoyed the admiring glances of the onlookers while he worked on me for four hours. It came as no surprise to find out that many of the tattoo artists were themselves living examples of their art and that they'd willed their skins to a Japanese Tattoo Museum. After death, they've made arrangements for their bodies to be shipped to Japan, and the skin removed and stretched over wooden mannequins for display!

Well, since my partner quit on me, the canvases are rotting in a basement out near the Golden Gate, my truck may be sitting somewhere in a northern California redwood forest, and the other pieces are god-knows-where. If you ever come across them, drop me a postcard.

» *Stood Up in Arizona*

Most of my business is confined to the Eastern seaboard, fortunately, because I've found that trying to carry out a transcontinental engagement can be a horror and a half.

Let me cite just one experience. A traveling executive from California had seen one of my bands perform during a visit to Boston and approached me about having them play at his daughter's wedding—which, of course, was to be held "back home". As we worked out the logistics of ferrying the group out there, we found that the flight would involve several transfers, and the client assured me he would arrange to have the appropriate tickets waiting at each changeover.

Well, at the transfer in Chicago, everything was fine—the tickets were waiting for them, and they hopped on the next leg of the journey. The next switch was at Denver—fine, the tickets were also ready and waiting for them there, and off they headed for Arizona.

But … Phoenix, alas, was another story—no tickets! The band telephoned my client to see if he could straighten things out, but for reasons I've mercifully forgotten, nothing could be done. So, no band for the wedding (and no wedding for the band), and a long, discouraging trip back to Boston. (Since the buyer had the responsibility of providing the transport out to California, he assumed full blame for the foul-up and paid the band their full fee plus all expenses.)

» *Dan Brown, Pre-"The Da Vinci Code"*

There's probably just a handful of people who haven't read or seen Dan Brown's *The Da Vinci Code*, one of the best selling novels of all time. And most people know that Dan used to teach at Phillips Exeter Academy in NH.

But few people are aware that Dan had originally cast his sights on a music career, and I knew him not as a world-famous author but as a singer-songwriter. He lived in Exeter at the time and had a small recording studio set up in his apartment, where he produced personalized cassette tapes of birthday songs for kids, entertained at parties, and produced a very original album of children's songs called SynthAnimals. He also released several CDs for adults: *Perspective*, *Dan Brown*, and *Angels and Demons*. We became acquaintances and I added him to my roster. Occasionally we'd meet for lunch at Loaf and Ladle, a natural foods restaurant in downtown Exeter, or one of the other eateries in town. One day he showed me an ambigram (a word or phrase written so that it reads the same rightside-up as upside-down) for *Angels and Demons* and mentioned that besides using it on the cover of the album he was also intending to incorporate it into a novel of the same name.

And the rest is history. Besides *Angels and Demons* and the fabulously popular (over 80 million copies sold worldwide as of 2009) *The Da Vinci Code*, he also wrote *Digital Fortress*, *Deception Point*, and *The Lost Symbol*. I would guess that his days of singing at birthday parties are long over.

Years later, when Dan appeared in a London trial on a charge of plagiarism by Michael Baigent and Richard Leigh, authors of *Holy Blood, Holy Grail*, a close friend of mine who had been present at one of my lunches with Dan, came close to being called as a material witness.

I'll have to say one thing for Dan. He's a really nice down-to-earth guy, and if anyone deserves fame and fortune, it's him.

» *Other Celebrities I've Met*

When you travel the show-biz trail, you occasionally rub elbows with the stars, even if you're small-time by most standards.

Conventions are a good place for such encounters, and there I've met **Red Skelton**, **Simon and Garfunkle**, **Leonard Nimoy**, **Smothers Brothers**, **Autry Family**, **Harry Blackstone, Jr.**, and **The Amazing Randi**. Being a fan of magic, I particularly liked to hang around the latter two.

One morning, before the exhibit hall had opened for the day, I ran into **Harry Blackstone, Jr.**, and he took me over to his booth to show me his latest illusion: a large "gas-chamber-like" structure, inside which was a chair. As I watched, he entered the chamber and sat in the chair, which began to revolve. As I watched through one of the windows, his form began to fade until only the empty chair remained, still slowly turning. Then after a few moments, he began to reappear, until he became solid once again. The chair then stopped turning, and he got up, and came out of the chamber, smiling knowingly.

Another time, when I was with **The Amazing Randi**, he was demonstrating some close-up magic, and casually asked me for my wristwatch, an analog model. Taking it, he turned it over face down and announced a time, then turned it face-up, and it showed that exact time. He repeated this several times before handing it back to me. During our talks together, we discussed computers, which he found fascinating, and the occult, which he was most definitely against.

To me the most memorable thing about Mr. Spock (**Leonard Nimoy**) is how unmemorable he appears to be in public. He's come to Boston on several occasions, and he travels virtually unnoticed through the streets and byways of Beantown. I guess people don't recognize him without those little pointed ears. The first time I met him he was sitting over on the sidelines of an auto show, completely alone and ignored, and happy for someone to talk to. At that time, the

Star Trek television series was winding down, and the movie versions were still a ways off in the future, and he'd just come out with a book of poetry (not a best seller by any measurement). The second time we ran into each other was at an Artist's Ball at Boston's Park Plaza Hotel. He was in town with his one-man stage show, *Van Gogh*, and he'd stopped over just to see what was going on. Afterwards, he wandered through the hotel lobby, gathered together a few buddies (he'd spent his earlier years studying at Emerson College, and knew a lot of people around town), called out, "Let's go for a beer!", and strode through the door and out into the dark streets in search of a suitable watering hole—all without attracting any attention whatsoever!

And the most memorable thing about **Red Skelton** is that his hair didn't have a touch of red left—it was decidedly a distinguished gray, but he retained all the enthusiasm and spirit that had characterized his stage act over the decades.

As far as my own acts go, probably the only one that would qualify for celebrity status is **Barbara Autry**, half-sister of the famed Singing Cowboy and LA baseball team owner, Gene Autry. She does—what else?—a lasso and rope-twirling act, with her daughter, Joslyn. They're always a big hit at country fairs and festivals, and the Autry name still inspires hundreds of fans to line up for autographs after the show. As the act progresses, Barbara twirls larger and larger lassos, until, at the climax, she's twirling a circle of rope with a 70' circumference. Now that may not sound very impressive, until you realize how much a rope circle of that size weighs, and how much sheer strength and energy it takes to keep it floating above the ground. Barbara has retained the beauty and lithe figure of a woman years younger, and when she finally lets this giant lasso settle to earth, it takes her nearly ten minutes to get her breath back.

**Figure 7. Tom Elliott and "Advisor to
the Presidents" David Gergen**

I've also met my share of politicos, although they don't constitute a large portion of my roster. One time I hired **David Gergen**, "Advisor to the Presidents") for an annual Wall Street conference. He's been an adviser to four Presidents: Nixon, Ford, Reagan, and Clinton. In the Clinton administration, he was Counselor to the President and then Special Adviser to the President and the Secretary of State. Anyway, I was there that day to escort him into the auditorium, and was anxious to hear what words of wisdom he'd gleaned from his impressive years of public service.

96

Unfortunately all he wanted to talk was golf and where he might find the best courses in the area. He did give me one prediction however, that then-Senator Tom Daschle had the best shot at the White House. Even insiders can be wrong.

Here's How to Contact Me...

Do you have a specific question or problem, such as:

- I've been asked to come up with entertainment for an all-day health fair. What kind of acts work?
- One of my performers is thinking of developing a one-man-band act. How can he get started?
- I'd like to hand out some color postcards of myself. Where can I get some printed for a reasonable cost?
- One of my clients wants a crowd-drawing act for her exhibit booth at a high-tech conference. What kind of acts can be adapted for this purpose, and how do I customize the act to the product?

Whatever advice you need, call me or send me the details and I'll shoot back an answer as quickly as I can. Many times, I'll have the solution in my head or in my files. If your problem requires an "expert", I'll phone one of my contacts who's had experience in that area.

  If it's a simple question, or one I can't answer, it's *gratis*. If it requires some time and effort, there'll be a modest fee. My e-mail address is tme01@verizon.net, my phone is (781) 647-2825, and my mailing address is P O Box 540441, Waltham MA 02454-0441

The TEP Networking Service

There's an old saying, "You can't sell from an empty cart". And most of you will be starting out with just that–an empty (or nearly empty) cart. Of course no matter how long you've been in the business and no matter how many acts you handle, there's always be some client who'll ask you for something you don't have (it happens to me all the time, and I have well over a 100 acts in my "cart").

  Networking is one of the new "in" concepts—it simply refers to people with a common goal or interest mutually helping each other, trading information, opening doors, exchanging product or clients. Here's how we apply it to our business:

- If you've discovered a really unique act in your area that you think might sell nationally, send me a Performer Information Form, brochure, glossy, news clippings, etc., on them. I'll add them to my files and, together with other contributions, build a resource library of acts from all around the country. Remember—I said *unique*. Your average folk singer, clown, juggler, or magician won't usually qualify for that honor. Also, they must be available to travel and be very reasonably (should I say "low"?) priced, since travel expenses will have to be added to their usual fee. If the act protests, remind them that "exposure" can be as important as, and traveling to new parts of the country as rewarding as cash.

- If you need a particular kind of act that you can't find yourself, contact me. Be sure to be specific regarding what you want (but leave as much latitude as possible so we'll have a better chance of finding a match), the date/time/length of the performance, the maximum budget (for fee, travel, lodging, etc.) your client can afford, and any other pertinent details. If I or one of the other agencies has an act that satisfies your requirements, I will inform you and give you the particulars.

Generally, both agents will follow the usual convention of basing the commission on the commission schedule of the agent who's supplying the act and then split that commission 50-50. The reason the supplying agent sets the commission is that the agent and the act already have an agreement on such matters and that agreement should be respected. For example, if agent Jones (the booking agent) needs an Oriental juggling team, and agent Smith (the supplying agent) just happens to have such an act and normally takes a 15% commission from the act's fee, agent Jones will tack on a 15% commission to the price he quotes to the client. Afterwards, both Jones and Smith will divvy up the 15%, each getting 71/2%.

A small fee will be charged for these listing and referral services, to cover costs.

DISCLAIMER

Any agent choosing to use this referral service does so independently of Tom Elliott Productions (TEP). Suitability, availability, and fees, commissions, and expenses due each agency, and other contractual details are to be determined solely by the two agencies. Also, the delivery of the act and the payment of fees, commissions, and other costs to the rightful parties are the sole responsibility of the agencies involved. In any case where TEP is acting neither as the booking agency or supplying agency, TEP makes no warranties or other claims or guarantees regarding any act, agent, or client, and assumes no legal, financial, or other liability for damages resulting from non-performance, non-payment, personal injury, non-payment, personal injury, damages to property, or any and all other consequences arising out of such referrals.

Finale

Even if you have no problems or needs, I'd still enjoy hearing from you. In particular, if you have any comments or corrections to this book, some success story to tell, helpful hint to share with your fellow agents, or just an interesting or humorous incident to relate, I'd very much appreciate your sending them to me.

Meanwhile, my sincere best wishes for a happy, healthy, profitable, and exciting new career!

Appendix A
Printing

Every business needs printing, and talent agencies are no exception. In fact, outside of the talent themselves, printing (and postage) probably will represent your biggest outlay. You'll need stationery, envelopes, business cards, full-color brochures, postcards, mailing labels, and other items. This appendix suggests a few sources for these supplies.

BEFORE AVAILING YOURSELF OF THIS INFORMATION, PLEASE TAKE NOTE OF THE FOLLOWING:

- Neither I nor TEP has absolutely a financial interest in any of these companies, and we make all recommendations based on our knowledge and, in many cases, our own experiences in dealing with these companies.
- All prices are rough estimates and are current as of 2008. Shipping and handling costs are additional. Stationery (letterheads, envelopes, memo pads, etc.) prices generally include a 4-line imprint, in black ink, on 20 lb white paper, unless otherwise indicated. You can get additional ink colors and different papers, for an additional cost.
- Just because one company's prices are higher than another doesn't mean that the former isn't a perfectly good deal—the higher priced company may offer better quality, or be able to ship your order faster.

Before ordering, call or write for catalog and samples, or check their website.

Terminology

The world of printed goods, like other industries, has its own nomenclature, and below I've given some of the most common ones:

» #10 Envelope

Sometimes called a "business envelope", these measure 9.5"x4.5". They accept a standard 8.5x11" typewriter sheet folded in thirds.

» Business Cards

Usually printed on 3.5x2" vellum or glossy card stock. Enclose them in all your mailings, leave one when you make a sales call, pass them out at your exhibit booth, and tack them up on bulletin boards and other public places.

» Clasp Envelope

Either manila or white envelopes, 9x12" or larger. They enable you to send 8.5x11" sheets unfolded.

» ID Label

A kind of "return address" sticker, only larger, usually 1x3". It is useful for sticking on leaflets, brochures, and other pieces not otherwise imprinted or stamped with your name and address.

» Mailing Label

Also referred to as a "shipping label". It usually has an attractively colored border inside of which is printed your name and address at the top, and space below for typing in the name and address of the person to whom you're sending the letter or package. Use it when you're mailing large envelopes (such as 9x12" manila) or packages (such as CDs, promos, videotapes, etc.).

» Sales Sheet

Sometimes called a catalog or product sheet. An 8.5x11" sheet, with ad (full color or b&w) on one side, and (optionally) text on the other side.

» Self-Mailer (aka Tri-fold Brochure)

Usually an 8.5x11 mailing piece, printed on heavy stock, that can be folded in thirds, with one of the outside panels used for printing the mailing address and return address, thus requiring no envelope.

Suppliers

Personalized Envelopes
http://www.personalizedenvelopes.com/
500 #10 envelopes for as low as $35.00
General-purpose envelopes, letterheads, mailing labels, ID labels,

Color Now!
11542 Knott Street, Suite 7 • Garden Grove, California 92841
Toll-Free: 1 800 257-4968 • Phone: 1 714 894-7800 • Fax: 1 714 894-7755

http://www.colornow.com/
Full-color brochures, sales sheets, ad reprints, posters.

Paper Direct
1-800-A-PAPERS
http://www.paperdirect.com/
Full-color preprinted trifold brochure, self-mailer, letterhead, business card, and envelope designs to make your mailings look expensive and professional. They do not provide imprinting, but you can use these items in a computer printer, or send them to your business printer. Overnight delivery available.

RapidoColor
705 East Union Street
West Chester, Pennsylvania 19382
phone: 800-872-7436
fax: 610-344-0506
http://www.rapidocolor.com/
Inexpensive full-color postcards, sales sheets, brochures. Quotes available on request.

And here's my all-time favorite, able to handle most of your business printing needs:

VistaPrint
www.vistaprint.com
Premium business cards, websites, free logo design, checks, letterheads, folders, brochures, return address labels, envelopes, postcards, brochures, flyers, folders, hats, T-shirts, pens, rubber stamps, decals, notepads, calendars…and more! Truly one-stop shopping. You won't believe their low prices—premium business cards start at 250 for $19.95. Plus they give away more freebies than you would ever dream: free business cards, website design, rubber stamps, etc!

Appendix B
Ready-to-Use Forms

In this Appendix:

Here are some of the standard forms you'll find handy in your day-to-day operation. Feel free to use them as-is or modify them as you need to:

- Agency Contract
- Client-Supplied Contracts
- Client Information Form (CIF)
- Performer Information Form (PIF)

You can either use these forms as a guide in designing your own, or in the case of the Agency Contact Form, Client Information Form, and Performer Information Form only, you can reproduce them, replacing my agency's name with your own.

Study the contracts carefully. They're an education in themselves, and underscore the many, many details you'll be responsible for, from supplying the client with the requested number of posters or publicity photos to making sure the act checks in with the right person at the right time.

Agency Contract Form

Here is the standard contract I've been using for years, as it seems to be sufficient for all situations. For special situations and added conditions, there is a section called "additional provisions" (item #12), and you can always tack on a rider (supplied by either you or your client) if needed.

Agency Name
Agency Address
Agency Phone #s, email address, website address

☐ Purchaser's Copy
☐ Agent's Copy; please fill in, sign, and return no later than _____
☐ Performer's Copy

STANDARD CONTRACT AGREEMENT

The undersigned Artist(s)/Agent and Purchaser agree to the following terms and conditions for the engagement herein described below:

1.   Name under which ARTIST(s) operate(s): _____

2.   Name of PURCHASER: _____

     Address: _____

                 _____

     Phones: [_] _____ (work) [_] _____(home) [_] _____(cell)

     Email: _____

3.   Official Institution Representative: _____

4.   Agreed price: $, payable as follows:

     Deposit: $_____, payable to _____ and due no later than _____

     Balance of $_____, payable to _____

     and due on _____ .

5.   Performance day and date: _____, _____, _____

*6.   In case of inclement weather,

     ☐ Performance will be held at time and place as scheduled
     ☐ Performance will be relocated to _____
     ☐ Performance will be rescheduled for _____
     ☐ Performance will be canceled, and no fee will be due Artist provided that
        Purchaser personally contacts the Artist at the phone number given below
        no later than _____ on the day of the performance.

*7.   Performance place (include map/detailed directions) _____

_____

_____

*8.   Start time/Length of performance _____

9.   Arrival time: _____

10.   Rehearsal/setup time: _____

11.   Artist(s) report to _____ at _____ .

Figure 8. Blank Agency Contract, Page 1 of 2

12.   If riders or additional provision/conditions are to be made a part of this agreement, indicate below:

_____

_____

_____

It is understood that _____and the Artist(s) execute this agreement as an independent contractor and is not an employee of the Purchaser, and that the Artist(s) shall have exclusive control over the means, methods, and details of fulfilling any obligations under this contract, except for performance time(s) and minimum and maximum length of the act.

Artist(s) agrees to perform and discharge all obligations as an independent contractor under any and all laws, whether existing or in the future, in any way pertaining to the engagement herein, including but not limited to Social Security laws, Workmen's Compensation Insurance, Income Taxes, State Employment insurance taxes or contributions, Public Liability Insurance; and the Artist(s) will hold Purchaser harmless against any such laws as well as against all Union claims for welfare payments.

Artist(s) represent that in performing under the terms of this contract that they are not infringing on the property right, copyright, patent right, or any other right of anyone else; and that if any suit is brought or a claim made by anyone that anything in conjunction with the ownership or presentation of said act or appearance is an infringement on these rights. Artist(s) will indemnify the Purchaser against any and all loss, damage cost, attorney fees, or other loss whatsoever by reason of Booking Agency permitting or allowing the presentation of the act or attraction called for herein.

Any controversies arising between Artist(s) and the Purchaser pertaining to this contract shall be resolved by the Courts of the State wherein this engagement is performed.

The Purchaser, in signing this contract, warrants that he or she signs as a properly authorized representative of the institution.

Date: _____   Date: _____

ARTIST: _____   Contact Person:_____

Artist phone # [__]_____   PURCHASER: _____

Agreed to by Artist(s) or Authorized Agent: Agreed by Official Institution Representative:

_____   _____

Date sent: _____   Date sent:_____

Date to be returned: _____

Figure 9. Blank Agency Contract, Page 2 of 2

Single-Act Agency Contract

Note: Information filled in by the agent is shown in bold face type. The asterisked (*) items indicate information obtained from the client, and either filled in when you make out the contract or supplied by the client when he or she signs the contract.

TOM ELLIOTT PRODUCTIONS
P O Box 540441 Waltham MA 02454-0441 (617) 647-2825

☐ Purchaser's Copy
☐ Agent's Copy; please fill in, sign, and return no later than _____
☐ Performer's Copy

STANDARD CONTRACT AGREEMENT

The undersigned Artist(s)/Agent and Purchaser agree to the following terms and conditions for the engagement herein described below:

1. Name under which ARTIST(s) operate(s): **Andrew and Samantha**
2. Name of PURCHASER: **Herald School**
   Address: **1200 Trapelo Road, Waltham, MA 02453**
   Phones: **[617] 555-4455 x2259** (work) [ ] _____(home)
3. Official Institution Representative: **Chris Pentham**
4. Agreed price: **$350.00**, payable as follows:
   $350.00, payable to **Tom Elliott Productions** and due on day of performance.
5. Performance day and date: **WEDNESDAY, OCTOBER 15, 2008**
*6. In case of inclement weather,
   ☑ Performance will be held at time and place as scheduled.
   ☐ Performance will be relocated to _____
   ☐ Performance will be rescheduled for _____
   ☐ Performance will be canceled, and no fee will be due Artist provided that
   ☐ Purchaser personally contacts the Artist at the phone number given below
      no later than _____on the day of the performance.
*7. Performance place (include map/detailed directions) **Activity Center, Herald School, 1200 Trapelo Road, Waltham. Look for signs "Herald School" and "Waverly Redemption Center" and turn in that road. Take first right, go for 200 yds., then take first left, look for Activity Center.**
*8. Start time/Length of performance: **6:30 PM 1-1/2 hours**
9. Arrival time; **6 PM**
10. Rehearsal/setup time: **15 minutes**.
11. Artist(s) report to **Chris Pentham at the Activity Center**
12. If riders or additional provision/conditions are to be made a part of this agreement, indicate below:
Screen will be made available by purchaser for projection, but artists must supply slide projector if needed.

It is understood that **TOM ELLIOTT PRODUCTIONS** and the Artist(s) execute this agreement as an independent contractor and is not an employee of the Purchaser, and that the Artist(s) shall have exclusive control over the means, methods, and details of fulfilling any obligations under this contract, except for performance time(s) and minimum and maximum length of the act.

Figure 10. Example of Single-Act Contract, Page 1 of 2

Artist(s) agrees to perform and discharge all obligations as an independent contractor under any and all laws, whether existing or in the future, in any way pertaining to the engagement herein, including but not limited to Social Security laws, Workmen's Compensation Insurance, Income Taxes, State Employment insurance taxes or contributions, Public Liability Insurance; and the Artist(s) will hold Purchaser harmless against any such laws as well as against all Union claims for welfare payments. Artist(s) represent that in performing under the terms of this contract that they are not infringing on the property right, copyright, patent right, or any other right of anyone else; and that if any suit is brought or a claim made by anyone that anything in conjunction with the ownership or presentation of said act or appearance is an infringement on these rights. Artist(s) will indemnify the Purchaser against any and all loss, damage cost, attorney fees, or other loss whatsoever by reason of Booking Agency permitting or allowing the presentation of the act or attraction called for herein.

Any controversies arising between Artist(s) and the Purchaser pertaining to this contract shall be resolved by the Courts of the State wherein this engagement is performed. The Purchaser, in signing this contract, warrants that he or she signs as a properly authorized representative of the institution.

Date **July 12, 2008**
ARTIST **Andrew and Samantha**
Artist phone # **[617] 555-1032**
Agreed to by Artist(s) or Authorized Agent:
Representative:

_____

Date sent: **July 13, 2008**
Date to be returned: **July 30, 2008**

Date_____
Contact Person: **Chris Pentham**
PURCHASER: **Herald School**
Agreed by Official Institution

_____

Date sent: _____

Figure 11. Example of Single-Act Contract, Page 2 of 2

Multiple-Act Contract

Sometimes it's simply more convenient and efficient to use one contract for multiple acts, rather than make out a separate contract for each. In this case, I was on-site for the performance

---

TOM ELLIOTT PRODUCTIONS
P O Box 540441 Waltham MA 02454-0441 (617) 647-2825

☐ Purchaser's Copy
☐ Agent's Copy; please fill in, sign, and return no later than _____
☐ Performer's Copy

STANDARD CONTRACT AGREEMENT

The undersigned Artist(s)/Agent and Purchaser agree to the following terms and conditions for the engagement herein described below:
Name under which ARTIST(s) operate(s): **Leonard Solomon,**
Fiddler and Dancing Bear, Mr Balloon
Name of PURCHASER: **City of Waltham**
   Address: **City Hall, 610 Main Street, Waltham, MA 02453**
   Phones: **[617] 893-4040** (work) [ ] _____(home)
Official Institution Representative: **Jack Latham, Steve Killarney**
Agreed price: Leonard Solomon   **$xxx (for four hours)**
Fiddler and Dancing Bear **$xxx (for four hours)**
Mr. (or Mrs.) Balloon $xxx (for three hours)
Payment of **$xxxx.00**, due and payable by check to **Tom Elliott Productions** on the day of the performance unless other arrangements are agreed to in advance.
5.   Performance day and date: **SATURDAY, SEPTEMBER 6, 2008**
*6.   In case of inclement weather,
       ☐ Performance will be held at time and place as scheduled.
       ☐ Performance will be relocated to _____
       ☑ Performance will be rescheduled for Saturday, September 13, 2008
       ☐ Performance will be canceled, and no fee will be due Artist provided that
       ☐ Purchaser personally contacts the Artist at the phone number given below
         no later than_____on the day of the performance.
*7.   Performance place (include map/detailed directions) **Front of City Hall, on Main**
     Street, Route 20, Waltham MA
*8.   Start time/Length of performance: **See above**
9.   Arrival time: **8:45 AM**
10.   Rehearsal/setup time: **15 minutes**.
11.   Artist(s) report to **Jack Latham, in front of City Hall**
12.   If riders or additional provision/conditions are to be made a part of this agreement, indicate below:
Raised platform will be provided by purchaser.

It is understood that TOM ELLIOTT PRODUCTIONS and the Artist(s) execute this agreement as an independent contractor and is not an employee of the Purchaser, and that the Artist(s) shall have exclusive control over the means, methods, and details of fulfilling any obligations under this contract, except for performance time(s) and minimum and maximum length of the act.

Figure 12. Example of Multiple-Act Agency Contract, Page 1 of 2

Artist(s) agrees to perform and discharge all obligations as an independent contractor under any and all laws, whether existing or in the future, in any way pertaining to the engagement herein, including but not limited to Social Security laws, Workmen's Compensation Insurance, Income Taxes, State Employment insurance taxes or contributions, Public Liability Insurance; and the Artist(s) will hold Purchaser harmless against any such laws as well as against all Union claims for welfare payments. Artist(s) represent that in performing under the terms of this contract that they are not infringing on the property right, copyright, patent right, or any other right of anyone else; and that if any suit is brought or a claim made by anyone that anything in conjunction with the ownership or presentation of said act or appearance is an infringement on these rights. Artist(s) will indemnify the Purchaser against any and all loss, damage cost, attorney fees, or other loss whatsoever by reason of Booking Agency permitting or allowing the presentation of the act or attraction called for herein.

Any controversies arising between Artist(s) and the Purchaser pertaining to this contract shall be resolved by the Courts of the State wherein this engagement is performed. The Purchaser, in signing this contract, warrants that he or she signs as a properly authorized representative of the institution.

Date __**July 12, 2008**__
ARTIST __**F&DB, LS, Mr B.**__
Artist phone # __**[781] 555-3339**__
Agreed to by Artist(s) or Authorized Agent:
Representative: _____
Date sent: __**July 13, 2008**__
Date to be returned: __**July 30, 2008**__

Date _____
Contact Person: __**Jack Latham**__
PURCHASER: __**City of Waltham**__
Agreed by Official Institution
_____
Date sent: _____

Figure 13. Example of Multiple-Act Agency Contract, Page 2 of 2

Client-Supplied Contracts

As I mentioned before, sometimes the purchaser insists on supplying the contract for a performance, so I thought I'd show samples of a few contracts I've received from clients over the years. They tend to be quite a bit lengthier than mine, but there are few surprises.

» *Simple Client-Supplied Contract*

Here is a fairly simple contract, one that's even shorter than mine! Contracts don't have to be complicated, and only the truly paranoid (or those who represent 7-figure acts) insist on 10-page agreements. This simple contract is the kind you might expect from retail establishments, public grade schools, clubs, civic organizations, and the like.

CONTRACT

This is an agreement between _____, who resides at
_____, herein called the
"Contractor" and the East Overshoe YMCA, 444 Park Avenue, East Overshoe, WI 05567.

1. The contractor agrees to provide _____ to YMCA members at a mutually
agreed upon time at the East Overshoe YMCA.

2. For above services, the YMCA agrees to pay the Contractor $_____. Payment will be
made upon receipt of an invoice from the Contractor following completion of services. Payment
of all fees is subject to previously agreed upon attendance. [Note: Although rarely the case, some
performance fees may be based on actual attendance at an event. This is particularly true of small
coffeehouses and other concert-type facilities, where an admission fee is being charged at the
door, so that the artist is actually getting a percentage of the "gross".]

3. The Contractor and YMCA agree that the Contractor is not considered an employee of the
YMCA, and will not receive fringe benefits of YMCA employees, and will not be covered by
Workingmen's Compensation, Disability, or Unemployment Insurance.

4. The YMCA will not make deductions for FICA, Federal, State, or City taxes from its
payments to the Contractor, but will report such earnings consistent with existing laws at the
time of this agreement. [A good point to remember: artists almost always owe self-employment
tax and all federal and state taxes on their earnings, and usually must make quarterly estimated
tax payments to the various governments.]

5. The agreed upon work for the Contractor is:
_____
_____
_____

6. This agreement is subject to economic, political, and natural events, and any other event
beyond the control of the YMCA, and may be terminated upon two weeks' written notice to
either party.

_____   _____
Contractor   Program Director, YMCA
Contract # _____   Date: _____

Figure 14. Example of Simple Client-Supplied Contract

» *Typical College/School Contract*

The contract shown below is a typical college or school contract, and contains clauses culled
from a variety of such contracts I've received over the years. (To my knowledge, there is no such
institution as East Jersey State College.). As you can see, colleges and universities probably have
a staff of legal beagles to come up with a complex document like this.

EAST JERSEY STATE COLLEGE
CONTRACT

This contract is between _____, hereafter called the "Artist", and East Jersey State College.

1.   The Artist or his Agent must wire or call East Jersey State College at telephone number (908) 555-1212 between the hours of 8AM and 4PM on the day preceding the performance stating the time of arrival, where staying, mode of transportation, name of person in whose name the group will be registering, and expected time of arrival of materials and crews. If any unavoidable delay is incurred in the arrival, the Artist or his Agent must call the above named persons(s) so that announcements can be made.

2.   If a rehearsal is not required, the Artist must make his whereabouts known to the Presenter ninety (90) minutes prior to the scheduled performance time and must be at the performance site at least sixty (60) minutes prior to the scheduled start of the performance.

3.   The performance(s) shall be held on _____, _____, 20__, at
_____.

4.   The Artist shall perform ____ show(s), each show being at least ___ minutes in length, exclusive of intermission(s) and the first show will begin at _____.

5.   The Artist shall limit his "break time" to no more than 15 minutes per hour of engagement period, such break times not to be consecutive.

6.   If the Artist arrives at the performance site noticeably under the influence of intoxicating beverages, narcotics, or drugs, the Presenter may cancel this contract with no liability on the part of the Presenter.

7.   Transportation and housing arrangements will be made by the Artist unless otherwise specified in this contract.

8.   (If the Artists contracted herein is an orchestra, only the leader must be specified in this clause.) The Artist _____ is in reality a group consisting of the following principals: _____
_____
_____

Since the essence of this contract concerns these specific individuals, and their personalities and talents which are recognized as unique, the Presenter will pay the fee specified in this contract only if the Artist performing is in fact the Artist agreed upon. If in the case of a group, the entire group does not perform or if the Artist is not the Artist specified in this contract, payment of the fee will be withheld until an adjustment is made between the Presenter and the Artist or his Agent.

9.   (This clause is applicable only if the Artist contracted is a band or orchestra.) If, for any reason, less than the specified number of Artists perform, action will be taken as follows:

A. If the headliner is, for any reason, not able to perform as required in this contract, the Presenter must be notified as soon as such a situation becomes known. The Presenter shall have the option of either canceling the contract with a full refund of any deposits paid and no liability, or of allowing the Artists to perform at a lower fee with an acceptable substitute.

B. If any Artist not covered in Part A is not, for any reason, able to perform, the fee shall be reduced an appropriate percentage (based on local union scale). Specifically, if a contract calls for seven musicians and only six perform, one-seventh (1/7) of the total wages due to these Artists shall be withheld.

C. Any substitutions must be approved by the Presenter in advance of the performance.

Figure 15. Example of Typical School/College Contract, Page 1 of 5

10.   If more than one act is part of this contract, the following provisions shall apply:

A. The headliner is to perform at least _____ minutes which is to include _____, _____ show(s).

B. It is agreed that if supporting act(s) is/are not listed in the attached contract, then notification of the exact nature of same must be received in writing by the Presenter at least _____ prior to the first performance contemplated herein.

11.   No deposits or advance payments shall be made prior to the first performance if the contract is signed by a properly authorized official of the school.

12.   In accordance with the policy of East Jersey State College, payment will be made by school checks to the Artist on the night of the performance. Two checks will be made, each for 50% of the total fee. If all conditions of the contract are not fulfilled, the contract will be renegotiated according to the violation and only one check will be paid to the Artist. The second check will be held pending financial settlement with the Artist's Manager or Agent.

13.   It is agreed that "papering" of the performance(s) contemplated herein may be undertaken by the school at any time during the ten day period immediately prior to the date of the opening if it is apparent that such "papering" will not decrease the opening night gross proceeds. In the event that "papering" becomes necessary to dress the house, the Presenter will contact the Artist's Manager or Agent for his approval at least ten days prior to the performance. [Note: "Papering" is the practice of giving out free passes in order to fill the house, especially on opening night.]

14.   The Artist agrees to furnish at his own cost the following amounts of advertising and promotional material, to the extent that the Artist or Artist's Manager has such material available for distribution:

_____ Press Circulars	_____ Ad Mats	
_____ Press Books	_____ Glossy Photos	
_____ Three Sheets	_____ Window Cards (posters)	
_____ Albums	this not being in excess of 10 cards for every $100 of Artist's fee.	
_____ Picture Mats	_____ Fliers, this not being in excess of 1 for each $1 of Artist's fee.	
_____ Other	_____ Other	

If neither Artist's Manager nor Artist has any of the above advertising and promotional material available for distribution, Artist's Manager shall notify Presenter of such fact within _____ days of the signing of this contract, specifying the item(s) which is/are unavailable. Failure to notify the Presenter indicates that all requested materials are available and will be supplied to Presenter. Because the parties recognize that failure to furnish this material will result to damage to the Presenter and will reduce the value of the performance, the Presenter reserves the right to cancel this contract if the Artist fails to deliver this material at least _____ weeks in advance of the performance. [Note: Ascertain prior to settling on a price whether the client expects such materials, and then add the cost of those materials to the fee.]

15.   It is agreed that all public performances by the Artist during the time period commencing 48 hours prior to the first performance and continuing 24 hours after the final performance in or about the city of _____ shall be approved by the Presenter. It is further agreed that the performance Is __ is not __ open to the public. In the event that the performance contemplated herein is open to the public, the Artist agrees not to give a public performance within a _____ mile radius of _____ three weeks before appearing at _____ without the approval of the Presenter. [This is an "exclusivity" or "non-competitive" clause to

Figure 16. Example of Typical School/College Contract, Page 2 of 5

Wait…there's more!

---

without the approval of the Presenter. [This is an "exclusivity" or "non-competitive" clause to protect the client from having his/her potential audience reduced by other appearances of the act.]

16.   In all cases specifying that the Presenter shall provide sound and/or lighting equipment, the Presenter's technical staff shall have complete mechanical control of the sound and/or lighting equipment.

17.   The Presenter is not responsible for any equipment not specifically stated in this contract. The Artist agrees that if he does not use the equipment required in this contract, he shall pay for all rental costs of said equipment.

18.   The Artist shall deliver a line plot and light plot, if applicable, to the Presenter at least four weeks in advance of the first performance so that the Presenter can advise the Artist or his Representative of the Presenter's ability to comply.

19.   If applicable to this contract, loaders and dressers shall be paid for by the Artist. ["Loaders" and "dressers" are extra stage hands required by the Artist.]

20.   The Artist must furnish the Presenter with a guest list no less than four hours prior to the scheduled start of the concert. The Presenter has the sole right to determine backstage access for all persons before, during, and after the show.

21.   The Artist agrees not to sell souvenir programs, books, photographs, or albums on the premises of the place of performance without the express written approval of the Presenter. If such approval is granted, East Jersey State College will retain 20% of the proceeds. [This is an important issue to resolve early during contract negotiations, as proceeds from such sales can be significant.]

22.   The Presenter agrees not to authorize the broadcasting, recording, or reproduction by any other means of that portion of the performance(s) or rehearsal(s) where the Artist is specifically involved. It is understood and agreed that this is a live concert, and that no recordings will be made.

23.   The Presenter shall not be responsible for any items heretofore mentioned when presented from doing do by an Act of God or any other legitimate conditions beyond the control of the Presenter. If such acts or conditions occur, the Presenter is not liable for any damages which the Artist, his group, or Representative might suffer.

24.   The Artist is at all times an independent contractor and not an agent or "employee" of the Presenter or East Jersey State College. The Artist further agrees to protect and save East Jersey State College, its officers, agents, servants, and employees, and each of them, harmless from any claims or causes of action of any kind or nature for mental or physical injury to person or damage to property which may be suffered or alleged to be suffered by any participant in the program.

25.   The Artist agrees to provide an Internal Revenue Service identification number or a Social Security number in the space provided in the signature block below.

26.   Union fees, welfare and insurance obligations are part of the cost of the production and are included in the compensation specified in this contract; therefore, the Presenter shall not be responsible for the payment of these obligations and the Artist or his/her Agent agrees to and shall hold the Presenter harmless from any such costs, fees, or expenses related thereto.

27.   Artist agrees to reimburse the Presenter for any damage caused by the Artist or crew.

28.   If for any reason, except due to an Act of God, this contract is canceled by the Artist beyond the cancellation clause contained herein, or a change of date is required by the Artist for any reason other than an Act of God, then the Artist agrees to reimburse the Presenter for his bona fide out-of-pocket expenses immediately upon presentation of a certified statement of such expenses to the Artist or his Agent.

Figure 17. Example of Typical School/College Contract, Page 3 of 5

And yes, even more!

29.   If this contract is signed by someone other than the Artist, the person signing for the Artist expressly warrants that he is authorized by the Artist to execute this contract for the Artist for this engagement at the time and place specified in this contract.

30.   The Representative of East New Jersey College in signing this contract warrants that he signs as a properly authorized representative of the College and does not assume any personal liability for meeting the terms of the contract.

31.   All additions and deletions in this contract and its riders must be initialed an dated by both parties to be valid.

32.   The contractor agrees and warrants that in the performance of this contract he will not discriminate or permit discrimination against any person or group of persons on the grounds of race, color, sex, religion, or national origin in any manner prohibited by the laws of the United States or of the state of New Jersey and further agrees to provide the commission on human rights and opportunities with such information requested by the commission concerning the employment practices and procedures of the contractor as relate to the provisions of this section.

33.   The Artist or his Representative stipulates that this contract is a valid instrument between the Artist or his Corporate Management and East Jersey State College. Intermediate agencies must be specified by the Artist or his Corporate Management on the following lines:

_____

_____

34.   The validity, construction, and effect of this contract shall be governed by the laws of the state of New Jersey.

35.   In the event of any conflict, inconsistency, or incongruity between the provisions of the Artists contract and/or rider and the provisions of East Jersey State College contract or rider, the provisions of the East Jersey State College Rider shall in all respects govern and control.

36.   The college will not sign contract or rider until the Artist or Representative has signed the contract, rider, and initialed all additions, deletions, and changes.

37.   To the extent permitted by the applicable State of New Jersey and college laws, rules, and regulations, East Jersey State College will honor the American Federation of Musicians (AF or M) contract terms as a courtesy, not as a contractual obligation.

38.   The action of East Jersey State College in returning said contract constitutes an offer to enter into an agreement on the terms herein stated, but unless said agreement is signed by the Artist on or before the _____ day of _____, 19__, this offer shall be automatically withdrawn without further notice and this contract shall be completely null and void unless otherwise agreed in writing by both parties.

39.   As the Presenter is buying a show and not the playing of specific compositions, and the Presenter has no control over which compositions are played, the Presenter assumes no responsibility for payment of fees, damage suits, or any other claims arising out of the playing of copyrighted compositions.

Furthermore, Artist understands that East Jersey State College does not hold a copyright licensing agreement with SESAC. Artist is therefore forbidden to perform any material that is copyrighted by SESAC.

Artist understands that failure to comply with the above mentioned clause will deem this contract null and void. Artist agrees to be fully responsible for any and all fees, fines, and/or expenses East Jersey State College incurs as a result of Artist's failure to comply with the above clause.

Figure 18. Example of Typical School/College Contract, Page 4 of 5

Getting dizzy yet?

ADDITIONAL TERMS:

1.   Artist agrees not to solicit funds while under this contract. [NOTE: This clause is specifically applicable to street entertainers. In this case, they are prohibited from "passing the hat" as is their custom. In other instances, we've negotiated the contract so that the artist can "put out the hat" in return for accepting a lower fee.]

2.   The Artist warrants that all music and vocals are "live" and that no recordings, lip-synching or similar methods will be used during the performance. [This has become an important clause since the late 1980s, when several Top 40 artists were found to have lip-synched during public performances, and refunds were demanded by the attendees, who had been led to believe that they had paid for a "live" concert.]

_____   _____
Presenter   Artist's Name

_____
IRS ID or Social Security Number

_____

_____

_____   _____
Presenter's Signatures   Artist's Signature
Director, Student   Comptroller,
Activities   Student Activities Assoc.

_____   _____
School   Person Signing for Artist

Figure 19. Example of Typical School/College Contract, Page 5 of 5

Client Information Form (CIF)

In each Client Information Form (CIF), which is recorded either on 81/2x11" forms, index cards, or in the computer, you should keep all essential information about each client or prospect, plus a running history ("Contracts") of all the acts they've booked through you.

CLIENT INFORMATION FORM

Organization: _____

Month First Contacted: _____ Source of Contact: _____

Name of Contact: _____

Address_____

_____

Telephones: _____(W) _____(H) _____(C)

Additional Contact Names and Phone #s _____

_____

_____

Possible Booking Opportunities (Dates, Budget, Types of Acts, Special Requirements):

_____

_____

_____

_____

_____

_____

Auto Message: _____

_____

Notes:

_____

_____

_____

_____

_____

_____

_____

_____

Figure 20. Client Information Form (CIF)

117

You might also want to record when ("Month") they do their scheduled bookings each year, so that you'll be reminded to contact them at that time. If you use a computer or word processor and produce form letters from time to time, you'll also want to store an individual message ("Message") to be inserted into the letters to make them more personal. Shown below are some samples of my CIFs:

Name of contact: Ms. Jo-Anne Hanson, Children's Librarian
Month: December
Organization: Agasset Public Library
Address: 750 Cooper Street, Agasset, MA 01999
Telephone: (413) 555-7991
Contracts: 20050219–Janice Blackman, Storyteller, for February vacation program. $250 for 1.5 hours.
200510903: "Shakespeare on Shakespeare" for Back-to-School opening. $450
Notes: Initially wrote me for information in October 2004. Budget is in the $150-$400 range.
Message: ".....entertainment for your cultural, school vacation, and other special programs."

Name of contact: Mr. Robert Elkovich
Month: February
Organization: US Expositions, Inc.
Address: P O Box 678, Cranston, RI 06999
Telephone: (203) 555-6393
Contracts: _____
Notes: Books for New England crafts fairs and expositions: CT 6/11-6/13, 8/27-8/28; Topsfield: 6/25-6/27. 2002: Expressed interest in Cheezo, Sgt Pepperoni, and David Tabatsky
Message: ".....entertainment for your upcoming Crafts Fairs"

Name of contact: Ms. Dorothy Shepherd, Special Events Coordinator
Month: January
Organization: Twin Tree Mall
Address: 5100 Old Worcester Turnpike, Framingham, MA 02345
Telephone: (508) 555-4150
Contracts: 20061203: Jester, Juggler, Roller-skating Santa Claus, 3 hours, $750.
20070409: Easter promotion. Robot Rabbit, 8 hours roving, $375
Notes: First contacted me in September 1989, asked for catalog.
Message: ".....entertainment for your special promotions during the coming year."

Performer Information Form (PIF)

Here is the Performer Information Form (PIF) that I use to capture essential information about an act I might encounter in my travels (I always keep a supply in my car). Since acts constantly change—in terms of personnel, repertoire, mailing address, phone number, fees, and options—it's a good idea to send out this form once every year or two to all your acts so you'll be aware of these changes.

(agency name)

PERFORMER INFORMATION SHEET

Name of Act: _____

Type of Act: _____

Main Contact: _____

Mailing Address: _____

_____

Telephone Numbers:　　(___) _____ (home)

　　　　　　　　　　　　(___) _____ (daytime/ office)

　　　　　　　　　　　　(___) _____ (cell/alternate)

Social Security Number or IRS ID No. _____

GENERAL AVAILABILITY (please describe in detail): _____

_____

_____

TYPES OF OFFERINGS: (e.g., roving/walk-arounds, 1-hour stage show, mini-concert, workshops, teaser plus stage show, etc.) Include a brief description of each, including the length of the performance.

1. _____

2. _____

3. _____

4. _____

CURRENT FEE SCHEDULE: (Please remember that the economy is rough and budgets are tight, so be realistic. Quote your lowest possible gross fees, from which an agency fee of 15% will be deducted.)

Performance Type (from above)	General	Schools	Colleges	Non-Profit	Other
1._____	$_____	$_____	$_____	$_____	$_____
2._____	$_____	$_____	$_____	$_____	$_____
3._____	$_____	$_____	$_____	$_____	$_____
4._____	$_____	$_____	$_____	$_____	$_____

Special Discounts for Block Bookings (Please describe): _____

_____

Are you funded? _____ By Whom? _____

Figure 21. Performer Information Form (PIF), Page 1 of 2

Additional Charges: Mileage: $_____ per mile beyond _____ miles.

Extra-Charge Options $_____ for _____

                               $_____ for _____

                               $_____ for _____

SITE REQUIREMENTS: (Please describe minimum stage area needed, including height clearances, whether you need or can supply a sound system and lights, and other mandatory requirements such as electrical outlets, dressing room, storage space, etc. Enclose a stage layout if applicable.)

_____

_____

_____

_____

CONTRACTUAL OBLIGATIONS: Do you presently have any exclusive contracts with other agents or agencies? If so, please list them, the markets (e.g., college) to which they have exclusive booking rights, and any arrangements you've made with them for booking through other agents (e.g., split commission 50/50):

_____

_____

IMPORTANT: Please send along one complete set of your publicity materials, a demo tape/CD/DVD, and any other information or materials you feel might help me better promote you. Thanks!

_____agency name/address/phone_____

Figure 22. Performer Information Form (PIF), Page 2 of 2

Appendix C
Sample Sales Literature

In this Appendix:

In this appendix you'll find sample form letters, data sheets, postcards, self-mailers, catalogs, and sample performer brochures.

Form Letters

Several times a year it's a good idea to send out a "form letter" to all your clients just to remind them that you're still around. For example, several months prior to the "big holiday season" is a good time to send a letter to all the retail establishments you deal with. For the college and school market, a letter just before summer, and another one in early September might be appropriate. (Note that this letter form is set up for a "list merge", where the word processor automatically inserts the name, company, address, and salutation for each client to whom you wish to send a letter.)

TOM ELLIOTT PRODUCTIONS
P O Box 540441
Waltham, MA 02454-0441
(781) 647-2825
September 1, 2010
<contact>
<company>
<address>
Dear <salutation>

Well, another year is beginning and you're probably in the midst of planning the entertainment for the fall semester.

As in past years, Tom Elliott Productions is ready and able to provide you with high quality, reasonably priced entertainment, with more than 100 of the most unique, memorable, attention-getting, and crowd-pleasing acts you'll find anywhere in the country. Just in the last two months, I've added a fire-eating unicyclist, a strolling gypsy violinist, and the cutest clown juggler you've ever seen, and I'm adding more new acts every month!

I can solve your budget problems, suggest how to inject new life into the same old program, and customize an act to your special situation.- I've been working with schools and colleges for over 15 years, and I know what works (and what doesn't)! I can put together an entire package—a 3-ring circus, an old-time vaudeville revue, or whatever, or supply just the pieces you need.

I'm as close as your phone, so give me a call at (617) 647-2825. If I'm out on the road, my trusty answering machine will take your message, and I'll return your call within 24 hours.

I've appreciated your business in the past, and look forward to continuing to work with you in the future. Please give me a call, and let me know how I can help.

Sincerely,
Tom Elliott

One-Sheeters, Postcards, Self-Mailers

If you plan to do a lot of mailings, you'll need to work up a standard "kit" of literature from which you can pull the appropriate pieces needed.

One piece might be a "capability" 1-sheeter, listing some of the clients you've worked with in the past. If possible, create a separate client sheet for each market, that is, one for colleges and schools, one for fairs and festivals, and one for businesses.

Note that just about any piece of literature can easily be adapted to fit a particular form. Just rearrange the photos and text, cut out a photo or two, and you can create a 1-sheeter, a post card, or a self-mailer (where you've designed one side to type in the recipient's address).

Tom Elliott Productions

Partial Client List: Festivals and Fairs

Over the past fifteen years, we've provided top-quality entertainment to many arts and crafts festivals and city-sponsored summer concerts and recreation programs around New England and across the country. Here are some names you're probably familiar with:

- WRKO's Londonderry Faire
- Wakefield Arts Council
- Mattoon Street Festival, Springfield
- Attleboro Summerfest
- Cambridge ARTICULTURE
- Salem State College Arts Festival
- SummersWorld, Worcester
- Levitt Pavilion for the Performing Arts
- Summerthing, Boston
- Lynn's Summer in the City
- DeCordova Museum Concert Series
- Marblehead Street Festival
- Charles River Arts Festival
- Norwood Summerfest
- Newton Summer Concert Series
- The Big "E", Springfield
- Arlington Town Day
- UMASS/Boston Harbor Festival
- Boston's 4th of July Festival
- Lagniappe Festival, U of S. Louisiana
- Children's Council Fair, Northampton
- Marlboro Labor Day Festival

In each and every case, we gave them great, attention-getting, crowd-pleasing acts–at sane prices! If your name's on our list, we'd appreciate working with you again this year. If it's not, we'd appreciate your giving us a chance to show our stuff.

Call us at (617) 647-2825 (round-the-clock answering service) anytime, and we'll return your call within 24 hours. Over fifteen years of experience in serving your needs, and over 100 professional acts–we've got exactly what you're looking for!

Figure 23. Example of 1-Sheeter

Sample Acts Listing

Another type of 1-sheeter is simply a list of acts you're currently representing. Again, this in an essential piece to stick in your mailing package.

Catalogs

Catalogs may be nothing more than a listing of your acts. However, some catalogs are much flashier and contain photos, printed in full color on glossy paper, and bound.

Performer-supplied Brochures

Many performers will supply you with their own brochures, but at times you may find yourself having to produce your own. Keep them simple – a 2-sided page is usually sufficient, but there may be times when you need a 4-pager. Color printing will often be beyond your budget, so stick to black-and-white if you can.

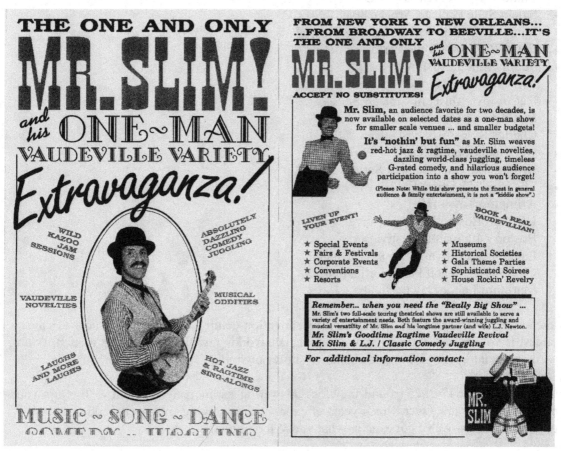

Front side   **Back side**

Figure 24. Example of 2-Sided Brochure

Remember to leave a space where you (or a sub-agent) can print, type, or stamp the agency's name, address, and phone #, etc.

Appendix D
"Yellow Pages" Listings

In this section you'll find a listing of many organizations that will be of help to you and your talent.

Note: All these organizations were extant when this book was being written, but some may have folded since that time. Also, names, addresses, and phone numbers may have changed in the interim.

Professional Associations

ASSOCIATION OF TALENT AGENTS (ATA)
9255 Sunset Boulevard, Suite 930
Los Angeles, CA 90069
(310) 274-0628 Fax (310) 274-5063
http://www.agentassociation.com/
Having been founded in 1937, ATA is the granddaddy of them all. ATA covers not only talent booking agents but literary agents as well. Their one-time application fee is $1000, and annual dues are based on your agency's income. Benefits, according to their website, include:

- Named Bargaining Partner for Guild Agency Regulations (WGA, DGA, AFTRA, & expired SAG)
- Interpret Agency Regulations
- Actor's Agent Search website – averaging 35,000 hits a week
- Settlement of Agency Commission Disputes
- Testimony and/or Present At Agency Arbitrations
- ATA forged alliances – this year's passage of the American Jobs Creation Tax Bill
- Informative ATA Newsletters on Website
- Round table discussions with your peers
- Monthly Board Meetings

- Educational Seminars (e.g., Understanding Collective Bargaining Agreements, Do's & Don'ts of Employment Contracts)
- ATA/SAG Residual Tracking System
- Membership discounts
- ATA/CSA (Casting Society of America) Cooperative Committee
- ATA/CCDA (Commercial Casting Director Association) Cooperative Committee
- Legislation
- ATA Full Time State Lobbyist
- Minors representation legal authorities
- Entertainment Health Care Insurance References
- WGA & DGA Outreach Programs
- Membership Meetings
- ATA Educational Contract Booklets
- Meetings With State Assembly Persons
- Meetings With Labor Commissioner and Legal Staff

The Music Business Registry, Inc.
7510 Sunset Boulevard, #1041
Los Angeles, CA 90046-3400 USA
818-995-7458 * Fax: 818-995-7459
www.musicregistry.com

A great source of invaluable directories and books on the music business, including *A&R Registry*, a bimonthly publication listing all the major contacts at record companies, *Film & Television Music Guide*, "the only directory of its kind and THE book if you want to get your music into film or television", *Music Publisher Registry, Music Attorney, Legal and Business Affairs Guide, Producer Registry, International Showcase, The Music Business Guide, Contracts for the Music Industry, Guide to Releasing Independent Records, How To Get A Record Deal, The Indie Bible, I AM a Professional Artist - The Key To Survival And Success in the World of The Arts, The Complete Guide to Starting a Record Company*, and *The Musician's Handbook..*

Fair and Festivals Associations (partial listing)

Check your local telephone book for the Fair and Festival association(s) in your county, state, and/or region. Many provide free online access to listings of fair dates and contacts. But what's most important to you as a talent agent is that many of their conventions provide an opportunity to showcase your acts for consideration as entertainment for the forthcoming fair(s). Note that almost all conventions are held either immediately after the fair season (October – December), or at the very beginning of the year in January.

- Association of Alabama Fairs
- Indiana Association of County and District Fairs, annual convention in January
- International Association of Fairs and Expositions, annual convention and tradeshow in December (see below)
- Kansas Fairs Association, annual convention in January
- Kentucky Association of Fairs and Horseshows, annual convention in January

- Massachusetts Agricultural Fairs Association, annual convention in November
- Michigan Association of Fairs and Exhibitions (MAFE), annual convention in January
- North Carolina Association of Agricultural Fairs, annual convention in January
- North Dakota Association of Fairs, annual meeting in November
- Ohio Fair Managers Association, annual convention in January
- Oklahoma Association of Fairs and Festivals (OAFF), annual convention in February
- Oregon Fairs Association, annual convention in January
- Rocky Mountain Association of Fairs (RMAF), annual convention in November
- South Carolina Association of Fairs, annual convention (with North Carolina) in January
- South Dakota Association of Fairs and Celebrations, annual convention in November
- Texas Association of Fairs and Events, annual convention in January
- Virginia Association of Fairs (VAF), annual convention in January
- Washington Festival and Events Association, (includes the Northwest Festivals and Events Conference in March)
- West Virginia Association of Fairs and Festivals (WVAFF)
- Western Fairs Association (California), annual convention in January
- Wisconsin Association of Fairs, annual convention in January

Other Entertainment Associations

INTERNATIONAL ASSOCIATION OF AMUSEMENT PARKS AND ATTRACTIONS (IAAPA)
1448 Duke Street
Alexandria, VA 22314 USA
Telephone: (USA) +1 703/836-.4800
Fax on Demand: (USA) +1 703/836-9678
http://www.iaapa.org
Founded in 1918, IAAPA is the largest international trade association for permanently situated amusement facilities worldwide. The organization represents more than 4,500 facility, supplier, and individual members from more than 90 countries. IAAPA strives to help members improve their efficiency, marketing, safety, and profitability while maintaining the highest possible professional standards in the industry. Publishes "Family Entertainment Centers Magazine" (quarterly): "Fun World"; "International Buyer's Guide" (membership directory, annual). Holds world-wide conventions and tradeshows, with the US version held in November.

INTERNATIONAL ASSOCIATION OF AUDITORIUM MANAGERS (IAAM)
Executive Director
635 Fritz Dr. Suite 100 Coppell, TX 75019-4442 USA
Phone: 972/906-7441 Fax: 972/906-7418
http://www.iaam.org

"IAAM News" (monthly); "IAAM Membership Directory" (annual). Holds international conventions and tradeshows annually, with the US version held usually in July.

INTERNATIONAL ASSOCIATION OF FAIRS AND EXPOSITIONS (IAFE)
3043 E. Cairo, Springfield, MO 65802 USA
PO Box 985, Springfield, MO 65801 USA
Phone: 417-862-5771 or toll free: 800-516-0313 Fax: 417-862-0156
http://www.fairsandexpos.com
Web site questions/comments: rachels@fairsandexpos.com
"Fairs and Expositions" (calendar of events, 10/yr.); "IAFE Membership Directory" (annual). Holds annual convention and trade show, in Las Vegas NV the first week after Thanksgiving.

INTERNATIONAL SOCIETY OF PERFORMING ARTS FOUNDATION (ISPA)
305 7th Ave., 5th Floor
New York, NY 10001-6008
Phone: (212).206.8490 Fax (212).206.8603
http://www.ispa.org
ISPA is a not-for-profit international organization (founded 1949) of over 600 executives and directors of concert and performance halls, festivals, performing companies, and artist competitions; government cultural officials; artists' managers; and other interested parties with a professional involvement in the performing arts from more than 50 countries in every region of the world, and in every arts discipline. The purpose of ISPA is to develop, nurture, energize and educate an international network of arts leaders and professionals who are dedicated to advancing the field of the performing arts.

NATIONAL ASSOCIATION FOR CAMPUS ACTIVITIES (NACA)
13 Harbison Way
Columbia SC 29211
Phone: (803) 732-6222 Fax: (803) 749-1047
http://www.naca.org
If you want to reach the college market, there are no two ways about it, you gotta belong to the NACA. Hosts about a dozen regional conventions each semester, plus an annual national convention in February, for campus activities directors from the US and Canadian colleges and universities. Each convention features an exhibit hall and a talent showcase. NACA was the originator of the "Block booking" concept, whereby several colleges in one geographical area each agree to book an act during the same week; in return, the act offers a discount price since travel and lodging costs can be shared among all of them (thus, schools who otherwise could not afford to bring in an act on their own can now do so). "Campus Activities Programming Magazine"; "NACA Membership Directory" (semi-annual); "Programmers Handbook".

Business Associations

NATIONAL ASSOCIATION OF THE SELF-EMPLOYED
P.O. Box 612067

DFW Airport, TX 75261-206
Phone: (800) 232-6273 Fax: (800) 551-4446
http://www.nase.org
The NASE was founded in 1981 to provide day-to-day support, benefits and consolidated buying power that traditionally had been available only to large corporations. Today, the NASE represents hundreds of thousands of entrepreneurs and micro-businesses. Specifically, the aim of the association is to help the self-employed successfully meet the challenges of managing and growing their businesses by: Securing focused tools and resources that help the self-employed manage and compete more effectively, representing the interests of the self-employed among legislators in Washington D.C. on key issues that affect their business and that give these businesses more equal footing with larger corporations, and providing access to benefits that promote the health and financial security of micro-business owners.

NORTH AMERICAN PERFORMING ARTS MANAGERS AND AGENTS (NAPAMA)
459 Columbus Avenue #133
New York NY 10024
http://www.napama.org
NAPAMA (North American Performing Arts Managers and Agents) is a not-for-profit association dedicated to promoting the professionalism of its members and the vitality of the performing arts. NAPAMA promotes the mutual advancement and the best interests of performing arts managers and agents; promotes open discourse among members and with the larger field; gives active consideration and expression of opinion on questions affecting the industry; disseminates and exchanges information through forums, meetings, publications, workshops, electronic media and new technologies; develops and encourages ethical and sound business practices. Annual conference in June.

NATIONAL CONFERENCE OF PERSONAL MANAGERS (NCOPM)
46-19 220th Pl.
11361 Bayside
New York, USA.
Phone: (718) 225-5103 (866) 91-NCOPM
http://www.cybershowbiz.com/ncopm
"NCPM Newsletter" (quarterly). Monthly meetings held in New York City.

SCORE (SERVICE CORPS OF RETIRED EXECUTIVES)
SCORE Association
409 3rd Street, SW, 6th Floor
Washington, D.C. 20024
1175 Herndon Pkwy., Suite 900
Herndon, VA 20170
Phone 1-800/634-0245 or 703/487-3612
Fax: 703/487-3066
http://www.score.org
SCORE, "Counselors to America's Small Business", is a nonprofit association dedicated to educating entrepreneurs and the formation, growth and success of small business nationwide.

SCORE is a resource partner with the U.S. Small Business Administration (SBA). SCORE is headquartered in Herndon, VA and Washington, DC and has 389 chapters throughout the United States and its territories, with 10,500 volunteers nationwide. Both working and retired executives and business owners donate time and expertise as business counselors. SCORE was founded in 1964.

Music Arrangers/ Composers/Songwriters

AMERICAN COMPOSERS ALLIANCE
648 Broadway, Room 803
New York, NY 10012
Tel: (212) 925-0458 Fax: (212) 925-6798
http://www.composers.com
As a non-profit organization dedicated to American classical music, ACA is a publisher, archivist, custodian, and concert presenter with a history dating back to 1937. Our catalog of works is one of the most unique and diverse collections of music in the world and includes compositions by Otto Luening, Vladimir Ussachevsky, Robert Helps, Dane Rudhyar, Karl and Vally Weigl, Halsey Stevens, Miriam Gideon, and many, many others

SONGWRITERS GUILD OF AMERICA (SGA)
(formerly American Guild of Authors and Composers)
www.songwritersguild.com
SGA Administration (Nashville)
209 10th Avenue South, Suite 321
Nashville, TN 37203
Phone: (615) 742-9945; Fax: (615) 742-9948
SGA East Coast (New York)
1560 Broadway, Suite 408
New York, NY 10036
Phone: (212) 768-7902
Email: ny@songwritersguild.com
East Coast Project Manager: Mark Saxon
SGA Central (Nashville)
209 10th Avenue South, Suite 321
Nashville, TN 37203
Phone: (615)742-9945; Fax: (615)742-9948.
Email: nash@songwritersguild.com
SGA West Coast (Los Angeles)
6430 Sunset Boulevard, Suite #705
Hollywood, CA 90028
Phone: (323) 462-1108; Fax: (323) 462-5430
Email: la@songwritersguild.com

NATIONAL ASSOCIATION OF COMPOSERS USA (NACUSA)
P.O. Box 49256, Barrington Station, Los Angeles, CA 90049
(818) 274-6048
http://www.music-usa.org/nacusa/
NACUSA is a 501(c)(3) non-profit organization. Founded by Henry Hadley in 1933, it is one of the oldest organizations devoted to the promotion and performance of American concert hall music. Many of America's most distinguished composers have been among its members. NACUSA presents several chamber concerts each year that feature music by its members.

Clowns

Check your telephone book or the COA website to find a local chapter.

National Headquarters:
CLOWNS OF AMERICA INTERNATIONAL
PO Box C
Richeyville PA 15358-0532
PH: (888) 52-CLOWN (724) 938-8765 (Outside US)
http://www.coai.org
The purpose of Clowns of America International Website is to share, educate, and act as a gathering place for serious minded amateurs, semiprofessionals, and professional clowns. COAI provides its membership with necessary resources that allow them to further define and improve their individual clown character. Visitors who are interested in the clown arts will find a variety of resources that will stimulate their interest, foster their curiosity and offer pathways to valuable information. They hold an International Convention every spring, usually located near a major US city. Members receive a bi-monthly magazine called *The New Calliope*. Check your telephone book or their website to find a local chapter (called Alleys).

Education

For a long while there were no schools that taught courses specifically for talent agents, managers, and the entertainment business in general, but recently I ran across something along those lines:

FULL SAIL UNIVERSITY
3300 University Blvd
Winter Park FL 32792-9862
(888) 993-7338
www.fullsailnow.com
I know nothing about their accreditation, but they are offering both a Bachelor of Science degree and a Master of Science degree in the Entertainment Business - online. Courses include Product and Artist Management, Negotiation and Deal Making, Mobile Marketing and Commerce, Business Plan Development, Advanced Entertainment Law. Campus programs encompass the music business, stage production and touring, and the recording arts. They claim to have been in business 29 years and to have graduated 27,000 students.

Funding

As a talent agent, one doesn't usually get involved in funding, therefore I've had little exposure to the subject. Generally speaking, it is the artist/performer or the sponsor (school, non-profit, etc.) who is responsible for obtaining funding for a particular endeavor. There are many agencies that provide funding for the arts, and the best way to research them is to Google either "government funding for the arts" or "public funding for the arts". The National Endowment for the Arts is probably the best known source, but there are hundreds of smaller ones lurking about.

Jugglers

Contact your local chapter of INTERNATIONAL JUGGLERS ASSOCIATION.

National Headquarters:
INTERNATIONAL JUGGLERS ASSOCIATION (IJA)
PO Box 7307
Austin, TX 78713-7307
http://www.juggle.org
The IJA is an organization of individuals dedicated to promoting juggling. Our volunteers make this happen. Members contribute to this worthy goal with both their time and dues. In addition members receive many benefits including: a yearly subscription to the IJA's official magazine (currently JUGGLE magazine), reduced prices on IJA videos, access to the members-only functions on this site, the right to attend the annual IJA juggling festival, and lots of other cool stuff. Also, many colleges have juggling associations on campus, and even though technically they're amateurs, some of them are surprisingly good!

JUGGLE, The Official Magazine of the IJA
Alan Howard, Publisher and Editor of JUGGLE
3315 E., Russell Rd. #A4-203
Las Vegas, NV 89120
Phone: (702) 798-0099 x107 Fax: (702) 248-2550

Legal Help

VOLUNTEER LAWYERS FOR THE ARTS
The Paley Building
1 East 53rd Street, 6th Floor
New York, NY 10022
Phone: (212) 319·ARTS (2787) ext. 1 Fax: (212) 752·6575
http://www.vlany.org
Since 1969, Volunteer Lawyers for the Arts has been the leading provider of pro bono legal services, mediation services, educational programs and publications, and advocacy to the arts community in the New York area. Through public advocacy, VLA frequently acts on issues vitally important to the arts community in New York and beyond. As the first arts-related legal aid organization, VLA is the model for similar organizations around the world.
VLA is supported in part with public funds from the National Endowment for the Arts, the

New York State Council on the Arts, a State Agency, the New York City Department of Cultural Affairs, and through generous gifts from law firms, corporations, foundations and individuals.

Magicians

Contact your local chapters of INTERNATIONAL BROTHERHOOD OF MAGICIANS and the SOCIETY OF AMERICAN MAGICIANS.

National Headquarters:
INTERNATIONAL BROTHERHOOD OF MAGICIANS (the "other" IBM)
11155C South Towne Square
St.Louis, MO 63123 U.S.A.
Office: (314) 845-9200 Fax: (314) 845-9220
http://www.magician.org
The I.B.M. is the world's largest organization for magicians and for people interested in the magical arts. Our Brotherhood is made up of nearly 13,000 members worldwide with over 300 local groups called Rings in more than 73 countries. The I.B.M. is considered to be the most respected organization for magic collectors, amateur and professional magicians in the world!

SOCIETY OF AMERICAN MAGICIANS
National Administrator
P O Box 510260
St, Louis, MO 63151
http://www.magicsam.com
The S.A.M. offers the opportunity to unite and associate with leaders in the World of Magic - not only professionals, but with amateurs, manufacturers, magic dealers, book authors and magic collectors. Through its monthly publications, annual conventions, and with over 250 "Assemblies" throughout the world, the S.A.M. provides the necessary forum for the advancement of magic through discussions, lectures, research, performances, and exchange of magic secrets within the magic community. To promote these endeavors the S.A.M. presents awards and fellowships in recognition of outstanding achievement in the Art of Magic. "M-U-M Magazine" (monthly). Hosts annual conference.

Mechanical Rights

THE HARRY FOX AGENCY (HFA)
601 West 26th Street Suite 500
New York, NY 10001
Telephone: (212) 834-0100 Fax: (646) 487-6779
http://www.harryfox.com
HFA is the foremost mechanical licensing, collections, and distribution agency for U.S. music publishers. Our processes, culture, and technology are client-driven and results-oriented. We continually strive to add value and strength to the music rights industry.
In 1927, the National Music Publisher's Association established HFA to act as an information source, clearinghouse and monitoring service for licensing musical copyrights. Since its founding,

HFA has provided efficient and convenient services for publishers, licensees, and a broad spectrum of music users.

With its current level of publisher representation, HFA licenses the largest percentage of the mechanical and digital uses of music in the United States on CDs, digital services, records, tapes and imported phonorecords.

Music/Musical Instrument Groups

If you check the 9700 block of the Encyclopedia of Associations, you'll find more than 100 specialized groups, each devoted to a particular instrument or type of music. There are groups build around such interests as rock and roll, rhythm and blues, steel guitars, southern Appalachian dulcimers, trombones, reed organs, harmonicas, jazz, opera, Scottish harps, old-time fiddlers, drums, ragtime, and Norwegian singing. The ones shown below are a small representation of these:

AMERICAN ACCORDIANISTS' ASSOCIATION (AAA)
152 Home Fair Drive,
Fairfield, CT 06825 USA
Phone: (203) 335-2045 Fax: (203) 335-2048
http://www.ameraccord.com

AMERICAN GUILD OF ORGANISTS
475 Riverside Drive, Suite 1260
New York, NY 10115
Telephone: (212) 870-2310 Fax: (212) 870-2163
http://www.agohq.org
Professional organization promoting organ awareness and education.

AMERICAN HARP SOCIETY
PO Box 38334
Los Angeles, CA 90038-0334
http://www.harpsociety.org
Grown from the needs of harpists - performers, teachers, and pupils, the American Harp Society is a tax-exempt, non profit corporation. Founded in 1962, membership in the Society is now over 3000 with chapters throughout the Americas.

CHAMBER MUSIC AMERICA
305 Seventh Avenue
New York, NY 10001
Tel: (212) 242-2022 Fax: (212) 242-7955
http://www.chamber-music.org
National association of professional chamber music provides links, calendars, email lists, publications, and grants.

COUNTRY MUSIC ASSOCIATION (CMA)
One Music Circle South
Nashville TN 37203
(615) 244-2840
http://www.cmaworld.com
Founded in 1958, the Country Music Association was the first trade organization formed to promote a type of music. CMA, originally consisting of only 233 members, now has more than 6,000 organizational and individual members in 41 countries. The objectives of the organization are to guide and enhance the development of Country Music throughout the world; to demonstrate it as a viable medium to advertisers, consumers and media; and to provide a unity of purpose for the Country Music industry.

COUNTRY MUSIC SHOWCASE INTERNATIONAL (CMSI)
P O Box 368
Carlisle IA 50047
(515) 989-3748
http://www.cmshowcase.org/

JAZZ WORLD SOCIETY ONLINE
P O Box 777
Times Square Station
New York, NY 10108
(212) 581-7188
http://www.jazzsociety.com/
The goal of Jazz World Society Online is to bring together jazz professionals - musicians, composers, record producers, distributors, collectors, journalists and individuals - to actively participate in the support and proliferation of jazz music.

INTERNATIONAL SOCIETY OF BASSISTS (ISB)
14070 Proton Rd. Suite 100
Dallas, TX 75244
Phone (972) 233-9107 Fax (972) 490-4219
http://www.isbworldoffice.com/ Email: info@isbworldoffice.com
The International Society of Bassists was founded by the world-renowned virtuoso Gary Karr in 1967. With nearly 3,000 members in over 40 countries, the ISB publishes a triannual magazine, *Bass World*, with an eclectic mix of articles about soloists, jazz and orchestral players, early music, pedagogy, international personalities and orchestras and reviews of new print music and recordings. News about upcoming ISB events and competitions and basses for sale is published in our biannual newsletter, *The Bass Line*. Every two years the ISB holds an international convention at a host university. Bassists of all ages and abilities come to enjoy a full week of workshops, masterclasses, recitals and lectures, and to shop in the exhibit hall. The ISB is a worldwide forum for double bassists to learn and share.

NATIONAL FLUTE ASSOCIATION
The National Flute Association, Inc.

26951 Ruether Ave., Suite H
Santa Clarita, CA 91351
Phone: (661) 713-6013 Fax: (661) 299-6681
http://www.nfaonline.org/

A not-for-profit institution, NFA is the largest flute organization in the world. It was founded to encourage a higher standard of artistic excellence for the flute, its performers, and its literature. Members include leading soloists, orchestral players, college and university professors, adult amateurs, and students of all ages. NFA annual conventions are held in major cities in the U.S.

BARBERSHOP HARMONY SOCIETY (SOCIETY FOR THE PRESERVATION AND ENCOURAGEMENT OF BARBERSHOP QUARTET SINGING IN AMERICA)
110 7th Ave.
N, Nashville, TN 37203-3704
Phone: (800) 876-SING 615-823-3993
http://www.barbershop.org info@barbershop.org

Music Publishing

NATIONAL MUSIC PUBLISHERS ASSOCIATION (NMPA)
Headquarters:
101 Constitution Ave. NW
Suite 705 East
Washington DC, 20001
Telephone: (202) 742-4375 Fax: (202) 742-437
http://www.nmpa.org/

The largest U.S. music publishing trade association with over 700 members. Its mission is to protect, promote, and advance the interests of music's creators. The NMPA is the voice of both small and large music publishers, the leading advocate for publishers and their songwriter partners in the nation's capital and in every area where publishers do business. The goal of NMPA is to protect its members' property rights on the legislative, litigation, and regulatory fronts. In this vein, the NMPA continues to represent its members in negotiations to shape the future of the music industry by fostering a business environment that furthers both creative and financial success. The NMPA has remained the most active and vocal proponent for the interests of music publishers in the U.S. and throughout the world, a continuing tradition of which the association is very proud.

Performing Rights Organizations

These organizations grant rights and collect royalties for the public performance of any copyrighted musical composition. This includes live performances, air play (radio and TV), use of music in a movie or other production, and the use of radio and recordings as "background" music in clubs, restaurants, lounges, etc.

AMERICAN SOCIETY OF COMPOSERS, AUTHORS, AND PUBLISHERS (ASCAP)
One Lincoln Plaza

New York, NY 10023
Tel: (212) 621-6000 Fax: (212) 724-9064
http://www.ascap.com
ASCAP is a membership association of more than 330,000 U.S. composers, songwriters, lyricists, and music publishers of every kind of music. Through agreements with affiliated international societies, ASCAP also represents hundreds of thousands of music creators worldwide. ASCAP is the only U.S. performing rights organization created and controlled by composers, songwriters and music publishers, with a Board of Directors elected by and from the membership. ASCAP protects the rights of its members by licensing and distributing royalties for the non-dramatic public performances of their copyrighted works. ASCAP's licensees encompass all who want to perform copyrighted music publicly. ASCAP makes giving and obtaining permission to perform music simple for both creators and users of music.

BROADCAST MUSIC INC (BMI)
320 West 57th Street
New York, NY 10019
(212) 586-2000
http://www.bmi.com
BMI is a performing right organization: It collects license fees on behalf of its songwriters, composers and music publishers and distributes them as royalties to those members whose works have been performed. As a performing right organization, BMI issues licenses to various users of music, including television and radio stations and networks; new media, including the Internet and mobile technologies such as ringtones and ringbacks; satellite audio services like XM and Sirius; nightclubs, discos, hotels, bars, restaurants and other venues; digital jukeboxes; and live concerts. It then tracks public performances of its members' music, and collects and distributes licensing revenues for those performances as royalties to the more than 375,000 songwriters, composers and music publishers it represents, as well as the thousands of creators from around the world who have chosen BMI for representation in the U.S. BMI currently represents some more than 6.5 million compositions — a number that is constantly growing. As a result, BMI has, over the years, sought out and implemented a number of technological innovations in its continuing effort to gather the most accurate information available about where, when and how its members' compositions are used as well as ensuring that payment to those whose works have been performed is made in as precise and timely a manner as possible.

SESAC (headquarters)
55 Music Square East
Nashville, TN 37203
Phone: (615) 320-0055 Fax (615) 329-9627
http://www.sesac.com
SESAC is the second oldest performing rights organization in the US, with headquarters in Nashville and offices in New York, Los Angeles, Atlanta, Miami and London.

Recording

RECORDING INDUSTRY ASSOCIATION OF AMERICA (RIAA)
1025 F ST N.W., 10th Floor,
Washington, D.C. 20004.
Phone: (202) 775-0101
http://www.riaa.com/.
The Recording Industry Association of America (RIAA) is the trade group that represents the U.S. recording industry. Its mission is to foster a business and legal climate that supports and promotes our members' creative and financial vitality. Its members are the record companies that comprise the most vibrant national music industry in the world. RIAA members create, manufacture and/ or distribute approximately 90% of all legitimate sound recordings produced and sold in the United States. In support of this mission, the RIAA works to protect intellectual property rights worldwide and the First Amendment rights of artists; conducts consumer, industry and technical research; and monitors and reviews state and federal laws, regulations and policies.

Songwriting (also see "Arrangers/ Composers")

SONGWRITERS GUILD OF AMERICA
1560 Broadway
New York, NY 10036
(212) 686-6820
http://www.songwritersguild.com/
Think of this as the songwriters' union, an advocacy group dedicated to protecting the rights of songwriters to profit fairly from their work. For the yet-to-be published writer, the Guild offers education, critiques, pitch opportunities, competitions, performance nights and other chances to hone and share their craft. For the professional writer the SGA offers assistance with publishing, royalty audits and collection, catalog administration, legislative advocacy and more.

Theater

NEW ENGLAND THEATER CONFERENCE
215 Knob Hill Drive
Hamden, Connecticut
Telephone   (617) 851-8535
http://www.netconline.org Email: mail@netconline.org
The New England Theatre Conference is a non-profit organization dedicated to providing its members with professional services, career development, and recognition awards in the live theater arts. Serving Connecticut, Maine, Massachusetts, New Hampshire, Rhode Island and Vermont, NETC proudly supports quality theatre and promotes excellence in all divisions of theatre. A recognized voice for practitioners in youth, secondary, university, community and professional theatre, NETC continues to expand its support of New England theatre in addition to nurturing and promoting.

THEATER COMMUNICATIONS GROUP
520 Eighth Ave., 24th Fl.
New York, NY 10018-4156
Tel: (212) 609-5900 Fax: (212) 609-5901
http://www.tcg.org
"American Theater Magazine" (monthly); "Theater Directory" (annual). Hosts biennial conference in June.

Appendix E
Bibliography

Since there are few courses available in this business, a good part of your education and training will have to come from reading, so do as much of it as you possibly can. If you're really interested in the entertainment industry, you'll find such reading not only profitable, but fascinating as well. There's no business like show business!

This is just a small sampling of the books and other resources available. What I suggest you do is Google (or Amazon) whatever you're looking for (e.g., "books on acting") and you'll find more than you can handle in a lifetime. Another great place to search is the For Dummies website (www.dummies.com) – I've included a few of them here, but they've published a book on just about every subject under the sun!

Those of you who own the original publication of *Clowns, Clients & Chaos*, will notice that many old standbys listed there – *Amusement Business, Directory for the Arts, Billboard's* fine directories, etc. – no longer exist.

Acting

Acting Skills, by Hugh Morisson
A & C Black Publishers Ltd, 2003. 192 pp. ISBN 978-0713664232.

Getting the Part: Thirty-Three Professional Casting Directors Tell You How to Get Work in Theater, Films, and TV by Judith Searle
Limelight Editions, 2004, 268 pp., ISBN 978-0879101947.

How to Get Work as a Movie Extra – 3ʳᵈ Edition, by Todd Worthington
Walkaway Entertainment, 1992,. ISBN 1-880255-01-4.??

Breaking Into Acting for Dummies by Larry Garrison
For Dummies, 2002, 360 pp., ISBN 978-0764554469

Your Film Acting Career: How to Break into the Movies & TV & Survive in Hollywood by M.K. and Rosemary Lewis
Gorham House Publishing, 1992, 296 pp., ISBN 978-0929149028

How to Audition: For TV, Movies, Commercials, Plays, and Musicals (2nd Edition) by Gordon Hunt
Collins, 336 pp., 1995, 978-0062732866

Advertising and Marketing

Advertising Age (weekly – 51 issues/year)
http://www.adage.com/
An weekly international business newspaper covering the latest marketing, advertising, and media news. Crain Communications. This is the "Bible of advertising".

Advertising from the Desktop : The Desktop Publisher's Guide to Designing Ads That Work by Elaine Floyd & Lee Wilson
Ventana Communications Group, 1993, 427 pp., ISBN 978-1566040648.
Illustration-packed pages showing you how to use your computer to save money on design fees, produce creative work, get expensive-looking art work for pennies, sell with ads, banners, and signs, and design attention-getting faxes.

ADWEEK (weekly – 36 issues/year)
http://www.adweek.com
Six regional editions. Similar to *Advertising Age*, except smaller and more regionalized. May offer free trial subscription to qualified people. Published by Nielsen Company. .

Guerrilla Marketing, 4th edition: Easy and Inexpensive Strategies for Making Big Profits from Your Small Business by Jay Conrad Levinson
Houghton Mifflin, 2007, 384 pp., ISBN 978-0618785919

Direct Marketing: Strategy, Planning, Execution (4th Edition), by Edward Nash
McGraw Hill. 200, 600 pp., ISBN: 978-0071352871.
Best techniques for getting faster action from direct mail and telemarketing.

Marketing With Newsletters: How to Boost Sales, Add Members & Raise Funds With a Print, Fax, E-Mail, Web Site or Postcard Newsletter by Elaine Floyd
EF Communications, 2003, 288 pp., ISBN 978-1930500112
How to write and design your own "talent agency newsletter" to inspire your clients to buy more. Explains how to decide if the newsletter approach is right for you, how to get other people to writer for it, how to target prospects, how to avoid copyright conflicts, and how to use shortcuts to save time and money.

Book Publishing

Boy, has self-publishing changed since I released the first edition of this book back in 1983! Back then, your only recourse was to go to a 'vanity press' publisher and pay good money to have them print a couple thousand copies (at a couple thousand dollars) in advance. And there they sat until you managed to sell them (storage fees additional)

Today, you pay a modest sum (around $600-900) to iUniverse or Xlibris or some similar firm, they lay out your book and enter it into their electronic database, and print copies only as needed. Promotional packages and editorial assistance are available at an additional cost if needed. What could be simpler?

Instant Book Writing Kit - How To Write, Publish and Market Your Own Money-Making Book (or eBook) Online - Revised Edition by Shaun Fawcett
2008, 180 pp., ISBN 978-0978170080

How to Self-Publish & Market Your Own Book: A Simple Guide for Aspiring Writers by Mack E. Smith and Sara Freeman Smith
    U.P. Gems Group Inc., 2006, 272 pp., ISBN 978-0966232882

Dan Poynter's Self-Publishing Manual, 16th Edition: How to Write, Print and Sell Your Own Book (Self Publishing Manual)
Para Publishing, 2007, 463 pp., ISBN 978-1568601427

Client Sources

With the disappearance of *Amusement Business* publications, many of the directories of yesteryear such as *Directory of North American Fairs, Festivals, and Expositions, Directory of Fun Parks and Attractions*, and *Trade Show and Convention Guide* no longer exist, but you can find online counterparts for many of these on the Internet. You can also check with local organizations (e.g., Massachusetts Agricultural Fairs Assocation - www.mafa.org/) for lists and schedules of fairs and festivals.

BackStage Online+Print
http://www.backstage.com/bso/index.jsp
Nielsen Business Media. Online and print source for finding jobs. Casting notices, production listings, auditions, and entertainment industry jobs for Film / TV Actors, Theatre Actors, Singers, Dancers, Models, Comedians, Staff / Crew, Writers, Musicians, Commercials, Reality TV, etc. Annual subscriptions may seem pricey ($135-$195), but if I were seriously looking for acting work, I wouldn't hesitate (monthly subscriptions are also available if you want to take it for a test drive first).

Directory of Fairs and Festivals
http://www.fairsandfestivals.net/

Directory of Theme and Amusement Parks
http://www.themeparkcity.com/USA_index.htm.

Directory of Renaissance Faires
http://www.faires.com/

Fairs and Festivals (Northeast and Southeast editions)
Arts Extension Service, Division of Continuing Education, University of Mass. at Amherst, Amherst, MA 01003. (413) 545-2360. A calendar of fairs and festivals.

Concert Promotion

How to Produce and Promote Small Concerts, by Jeff Brown
http://www.alaska.net/~jbrown/concert.html

Also, the NACA (National Association for Campus Activities) produces a number of booklets on the subject:
http://www.naca.org/NACA/PublicationsResources/

Direct Marketing

Most of your marketing efforts will be direct: you'll be contacting people who may be interested in hiring entertainment. Phoning, Emailing, and snail-mailing all share things in common, so you can apply many of these publications to any method.

Small Business Marketing for Dummies, Second Edition by Barbara Findlay Schenck
For Dummies, 2004, 384 pp., ISBN 978-0764578397

Direct Mail for Dummies by Richard Goldsmith
IDG Books. 2002, unknown pages, ISBN 978-0764507649.

The Complete Guide to Direct Marketing: Creating Breakthrough Programs That Really Work by Chet Meisner
Kaplan Business. 2006, 280 pp., ISBN 978-1419526930
Step-by-step overview of direct marketing from strategic approach to execution.

The Ultimate Sales Letter: Attract New Customers. Boost Your Sales (Ultimate Sales Letter) by Dan S. Kennedy
Adams Media. 2006, 204 pp., ISBN 978-1593374990
How to write letters that get read, generate leads, and make money.

Entertainment and Business (General)

Complete MBA For Dummies, 2nd Edition by Dr. Kathleen Allen
For Dummies, 2007, 414 pp., ISBN 978-0-470-19429-4

All You Need To Know About the Music Business: 6th Edition, by Donald Passman

Free Press, 2006, 464 pp., ISBN 978-0743293181
This, along with *This Business of Music* (see below), is another must-have for your library. Covers all the latest changes regarding CDs, Internet publishing, iPod sharing, etc.

This Business of Artist Management by Jr. Xavier M. Frascogna
Billboard Books, 2004, 304 pp., ISBN 978-0823076888

Columbia Journal of the Law and the Arts (quarterly)
http://www.law.columbia.edu/current_student/Law_Journals/law_arts
Covers the legal aspects of the entertainment business. Probably more than you really need to know, but it could be helpful.

Association of Talent Agents Newsletter (monthly)
Association of Talent Agents
9255 Sunset Blvd., Suite 318
Los Angeles, CA 90069
(213) 274-0628.
http://www.agentassociation.com/frontdoor/about_ata.cfm
Their newsletters are available online.

Billboard
http://www.billboard.com/bbcom/index.jsp
As most of you know, Billboard Publications – including *Billboard Magazine* – was purchased by Nielsen Company (http://www.nielsenbusinessmedia.com/)

Legal Aspects of the Music Industry by Richard Schulenberg
Billboard Books, 2005, 624 pp., ISBN 978-0823083640

Legal Guide for Starting & Running a Small Business by Fred S. Steingold
NOLO, 2008, 457 pp., ISBN 978-1413308532

The Music Business: Career Opportunities and Self-Defense (Paperback) by Dick Weissman
Three Rivers Press, 2003, 416 pp., ISBN 978-0609810132

This Business of Entertainment and Its Secrets
New National Publishing Company, 1985. 299 pp. ISBN 0-882806-02-6

This Business of Music, 10th Edition by M. William Krasilovsky, Sidney Shemel, John M Gross, and Jonathan Feinstein
I am so happy to see that this book is still in print. I bought my first copy back in the early 80s and that, along with a course I took of the same name, was my introduction to what the music business is all about. This is a must for your reference library!
Billboard Books, 2007 570 pp., ISBN 978-0823077236

This Business of Music Marketing and Promotion, Revised and Updated Edition by Tad Lathrop

Billboard Books, 2003, 308 pp., ISBN 978-0823077298
Includes completely updated material about Internet sales and promotion techniques, the latest information available on integrated marketing and e-marketing strategies, and brand-new listings of information resources.

Variety Magazine (Weekly)
Los Angeles: 5700 Wilshire Blvd., Suite 120, Los Angeles, CA 90036 (323) 857-6600
New York: 360 Park Ave. South, New York, NY 10010
http://www.variety.com/
Covers all of the entertainment business: TV, cable, film, theater, music, personal appearances.

Entrepreneurship and Business

Entrepreneur Magazine (Monthly)
A good review of what other creative types are doing to make money. Loads of "how to" articles, success stories, franchise profiles, etc.. Besides their flagship publication, they also publish magazines on Franchises and Business Opportunities, and there's even a magazine for female entrepreneurs. Also source of a host of how-to books and manuals about starting different businesses.
http://www.entrepreneur.com.

The McGraw-Hill 36-Hour Accounting Course, 4th Ed. by Harold E. Arnett, Howard Davidof, and Howard Davidoff.
McGraw-Hill, 2007, 416 pp., ISBN 978-0071486033
Befuddled by figures? Here are 36 separate 1-hour courses that teach non-accountants about cash flow, tax accounting, fixed assets and depreciation, working capital, and more.

Finding Money: The Small Business Guide to Financing (Small Business Series) by Kate Lister
Wiley, 1996, 256 pp., ISBN 978-0471109846

Small Business For Dummies (For Dummies by Eric Tyson and Jim Schell
Wiley, 2008, 410 pp., ISBN 978-0470177471

Small Business Financial Management Kit For Dummies by Tage C. Tracy and John A., Tracy.
For Dummies, 2007, 357 pp., ISBN 978-0470125083.

Adams Streetwise Small Business Start-Up: Your Comprehensive Guide to Starting and Managing a Business (Adams Streetwise Series) by Bob Adams
Adams Media, 2002, 416 pp., ISBN 978-1558505810.

SmartStart Your Own <name of state> Business, Ernst & Young Staff
Oasis Press and PSI Research, various dates. A 50-book series (one for each state). Comprehensive guides that include tax forms, applications and registrations, and tips on how to cut through the red tape. 250-400 pages/book. Various ISBNs.

Public Relations

Handbook of Public Relations by Robert Lawrence Heath
Sage Publications, 2004, 816 pp., ISBN 978-1412909549

Public Relations For Dummies by Ilise Benun
For Dummies, 2006, 384 pp., ISBN 978-0471772729

Public Relations: The Complete Guide (hardcover), by Joe Marconi
Southwestern Educational Publishing, 2004, 392 pp., ISBN 978-0324203042

PRWeek (online) http://www.prweekus.com/
A compendium of news on public relations happenings in the US; separate sites for other countries
worldwide. Free.

Radio, TV, and Album Production

Start and Run Your Own Record Label, Revised and Expanded Edition by Daylle Deanna
Schwartz
Billboard Books, 2003, 304 pp., ISBN 978-0823084333

Label Launch: A Guide to Independent Record Recording, Promotion, and Distribution by Veronika
Kalmar
St Martins Griffin, 2002, 208 pp., ISBN 978-0312263508

Producing for TV and Video: A Real-World Approach by Cathrine Kellison
Focal Press, 2005, 280 pp., ISBN 978-0240806235

Directing and Producing for Television, Third Edition: A Format Approach by Ivan Cury
Focal Press, 2006, 272 pp., ISBN 978-0240808277

Television Production Handbook by Herbert Zettl
Wadsworth Publishing, 2005, 576 pp., ISBN 978-0534647278
A workbook is also available.

This Business of Radio Programming by Claude and Barbara Hall
O Liners L a Air Force , 2000, 360 pp., ISBN 978-0970586414
A behind-the-scenes look at the world of program lists, top-40, ratings, and DJs. More of a history/
analysis of radio than a how-to book, but good reading for those of you who want to make the
music business a career.

This Business of Television by Howard Blumenthal and Oliver Goodenough
Billboard Books, 1998, 666 pp., ISBN 978-0823077045

Recording Business

The Real Deal: How to Get Signed to a Record Label by Daylle Deanna Schwartz
Billboard Books, 2002, 288 pp., ISBN 978-0823084050

Getting Signed!: An Insider's Guide to the Record Industry by George Howard
Berklee Press, 2003, 203 pp., ISBN 978-0876390450

Musician's Business and Legal Guide, (3rd Edition) by Mark Halloran
Prentice Hall, 2001, 489 pp., ISBN 978-0130316813

Sales and Marketing

How to Master the Art of Selling by Tom Hopkins, the Nation's #1 Sales Trainer
Business Plus, 2005, 416 pp., ISBN 978-0446692748 How to create the selling climate, referral prospecting, phone techniques, handling objections, power closes. Also: You can get Hopkin's course, *Audio Sales Collection*, on CD from WarnerAudio, ISBN 978-0060514716..

Selling 101: What Every Successful Sales Professional Needs to Know by Zig Ziglar
Thomas Nielson, 2003, 96 pp., ISBN 978-0785264811

Selling for Dummies, by Tom Hopkins
For Dummies, 2001, 384 pp., ISBN 978-0764553639

Talent Sources

Cavalcade of Acts and Attractions (Annual)
    This appears to have gone out of business as the latest issue I can find is 2005. Even an old copy may be of some use in tracking down various performers and their agents. The best available substitute is Billboard Publications' *International Talent and Touring Guide* (see below).

Celebrity Service International Contact Book
Celebrity Source Inc., 6255 Sunset Blvd., Suite 908, Los Angeles, CA 90028, phone (323) 957-0508. This annually published trade directory of the entertainment industry has now gone online with a database of over 650,000 celebrity contacts of actors, musicians, artists, comedians, athletes, media personalities, politicians, authors, and anyone in the public eye. www.celebrityservice.com

Circus Report (Twice monthly)
A great source of circus information, news, routes, data on show people, and reviews of shows and books. Annual subscription available through Amazon.

International Talent and Touring Guide (annual)
Put out by Billboard Publications, this is the premier global reference guide for anyone who books,

promotes or manages talent. The new 2009 edition is conveniently organized and completely updated with over 30,000 artists,managers and agents from 69 countries worldwide, including the U.S. and Canada. Includes contact names, phone & fax numbers, email and website addresses, artists and their record labels, managers and agents, tour services and merchandise, sound & lighting vendors, equipment & instrument rentals, limo rentals, security services and more, national promoters and their key personnel, and state-by-state venue reviews, with contact information and capacity listings. This is an all-in-one reference and well worth the cost.

Trade Shows/Exhibits

Remember: trade shows can be a two-way street: you can exhibit at trade shows to get more business, *and* you can also sell talent to trade show exhibitors to attract people to their booth.

How to Get the Most Out of Trade Shows, by Steve Miller
NTC Business Books, 2000, 161 pp., ISBN 978-0658009396

Biz Tradeshows
An online source of tradeshows scheduled in major countries and cities around the world. http://www.biztradeshows.com/

Trade Show & Event Marketing: Plan, Promote & Profit, by Ruth Stevens
South-Western Educational Publishing, 2005, 352 pp., ISBN 978-0324206241